PRACTICAL APOLOGETICS

A FAITH WORTH FIGHTING FOR

MARK MORROW

FREILING
PUBLISHING

Scripture quotations are taken from the
Holy Bible, New Living Translation,
© 1996, 2004, 2007 by the Tyndale House Foundation.

Published by Freiling Publishing, a division of Freiling Agency, LLC.

P.O. Box 1264,
Warrenton, VA 20188

www.FreilingPublishing.com

ISBN 978-1-950948-59-8

Printed in the United States of America

ACKNOWLEDGMENTS

Of course, a book of this magnitude could not come about by just one person. I am deeply indebted to the following people:

Pam, my dear wife. Thank you for allowing me the time and space to write this book. Every project "steals" from something else. As co-pastors of a large church and as co-parents of a large family, my work on this book required extra effort on your part to pick up the slack on all of our other responsibilities.

Don and Linda Morrow, my wonderful parents. Thank you for challenging me to read and process Josh McDowell's *Evidence that Demands a Verdict* when I was in high school. I may not have ever developed an interest in apologetics otherwise.

Alexandra Rutkowski, my talented assistant. Thank you for taking all my rough notes from years of lectures, compiling them into chapters, verifying all the sources, and correcting all my grammar mistakes.

Freiling Publishing, my amazing publishers. Thank you, Christen, for conducting the careful formatting and making this book in its presentable shape. And thank you, Tom, for believing in this project and for the interest and skill in coming alongside me to get this message out.

I feel like a dime among dollars, but I am humbly grateful.

TABLE OF CONTENTS

PREFACE

As I was entering public high school, my God-fearing parents were concerned that a constant exposure to a secular worldview could undermine the biblical truths that they had instilled in me up to that point. So, they presented me with Josh McDowell's seminal book, *Evidence that Demands a Verdict*. Of all the birthdays and Christmases that I have celebrated, that book was one of the best gifts they ever gave me. As an adolescent transitioning from coasting on my parents' faith as a child to having to work out my faith for myself as an adult, I devoured every single page as delicious morsels of truth. That book has gone on to become one of the most trusted sources for Christians in their attempt to equip themselves to defend their faith against the most strident critics and skeptics. In those vulnerable developmental years, I was thrilled to discover that all I had learned about Jesus and His Word can be verified by factual proof and sound reasoning. I could be both an intellectual and a Christian; faith and reason are compatible. Such a premise has served me well all of my life.

Sure enough, my faith was challenged by fellow students who relished in novel ways of thinking as well as teachers who seemed to be on a humanistic mission to excise God out of everyone's worldview. But because I had devoted myself to diligently studying apologetics, I not only survived high school, but I was also confident to counter the secular ideas swarming the public arena. And I was able to lead many of my friends to the truth that Jesus is who He claims to be.

A few years later as a youth pastor, I was dismayed that so many of the young people in our church were forsaking their faith after returning home from their first year of college. So, to equip students to understand and defend their faith before they graduated from high school, I began teaching high school students the ideas that I had had to develop and comprehend myself. I was determined to help students build a foundation for their faith and preserve their Christian worldview in hostile environments.

After years of honing rational responses to the Christian faith's common challenges, I was invited to teach those concepts in a collegiate setting. The local university where I lived had a practice of inviting China's brightest and most promising graduate students to learn advanced engineering concepts for a year as a part of their studies. But the administration was surprised to find that many of these students who came from a staunch atheistic worldview back home were inquiring more about "the American God" than they were about industrial science. Ill-equipped to handle the very tough, philosophical questions posed by these exceptional Chinese students, the administration tapped me to teach a religion class in which they could enroll. I not only had to write the course, but then I also had to answer all their questions each day. Compared to their IQ, I felt as if I was totally out of their league! My frequently used line became, "That is a great question, but I do not know the answer. Please come back tomorrow, and I will answer that question for you." Then I would spend sleepless nights researching answers that would satisfy the sharpest minds that I have ever encountered. These earnest seekers were not argumentative or indifferent; they just wanted the truth to make sense—truth of which they had been deprived their whole lives. I am glad to say that, with the Holy Spirit's help (Luke 12:11-12), I became quite adept at God's command in 1 Peter 3:15, which says, "If someone asks about your hope as a believer, always be ready to explain it." Many of those students came to a saving faith in Jesus throughout that course, maintained contact with me long afterwards, and returned to their homeland on a mission to spread the Gospel in their realms of influence.

Then as a dad, when my kids entered high school and college, I felt a grave responsibility to prepare them for the great challenges that laid ahead of them in a postmodern world that has grown increasingly hostile to the Christian faith. As they would come home with new questions posed to them by classmates and teachers, I continued digging for the truth as if I was prospecting for nuggets of gold. Today, all of my adult children have a solid faith in Jesus that is bolstered with sound reasoning, and they are unafraid of the many questions they face in their various contexts.

Since then, I have had the privilege of traveling worldwide and encountering many different worldviews. I have gone all throughout Eastern Europe—a former Communist region still steeped in atheism—lecturing and fielding questions convincingly about subjects like the existence of God, the trustworthiness of the Bible, the Lordship of Jesus, and the sensibility of creation. I have also traveled throughout India and Southeast Asia—a region characterized by mystical polytheism—speaking on topics like the exclusivity of Jesus and the value of pain and suffering. And I have gone throughout the Middle East and Africa—a region permeated by Muslim ideology—preaching on the grace, mercy, love, forgiveness, and the relational aspects of Jesus. Then back here at home as a pastor of a large, multisite church, I have also preached these concepts more than once to our very diverse congregation. Often, there have been those who took it upon themselves to fact-check in real time with their smartphones the points that I was making as I was preaching. If they had questions or if the information was not absolutely sufficient to them, then I would have certainly heard about it!

So, this book's concepts have been shaped by over forty years of the most rigorous testing from a wide range of environments. These ideas are not merely shallow, theoretical concepts borrowed from books and websites here and there without context and application. Rather, this defense of the Christian faith's basic tenets has survived the most daunting challenges by some of the most intelligent, inquisitive minds. Yet, the truths are also quite simple and, as one will see, can be easily explained in layman's terms.

May God use this resource to equip you with the ability to explain effectively the hope that you possess as a believer whenever someone asks you. After all, as a follower of Christ in this day and age, you will be asked. So, get yourself ready.

Mark

Introduction:

APOLOGETICS IN A POSTMODERN AGE

Truth is a casualty of our pop culture. The conventional wisdom of today appears to be a reaction to the assumed certainty of past scientific efforts to explain reality. Known as postmodernism, this ideology is slowly replacing rationality. People are becoming increasingly skeptical of explanations that claim to be appropriate for all people groups. Instead, they insist, each person has the right to their own interpretation of reality and truth. "Your truth is different from my truth" is often argued. Eclecticism has replaced the single paradigm or set of assumptions that most people in previous generations found common ground. As a result, such a worldview is significantly affecting morality, politics, business, education, economics, literature, art, music, media, entertainment, religion, family... everything. And woe to the one who attempts to impose what they believe to be true upon anyone else. There is increasing societal pressure to keep one's convictions to themselves. Thus, there is a present-day challenge for apologists in their attempt to defend the faith because the entire basis for common reasoning seems to have been removed by today's prevalent attitudes.

Or is it a challenge after all? Can one's reality be defined by their experience? Or is this faulty and self-contradictory view easy to dismantle by the astute apologist who has prepared themselves accordingly? Allow me to illustrate. In my lifetime, I have had the opportunity to observe many interesting sites all around the world. Yet, I have to admit that I have never seen the Great Pyramid of Giza. Apparently, it is the oldest of the Seven Wonders of the Ancient World. And I am told that it is a tomb that is located outside of Cairo, Egypt. However, I have never actually seen it, and I have no personal proof that it exists. Even so, my lack of experiencing this ancient landmark does not change its reality. It has a specific history that exists outside of my familiarity. This amazing artifact exists whether I accept or reject that it does.

A suggestion that either wind patterns or aliens from outer space could have been responsible for this pyramid's intricate design and construction instead of brilliant Egyptian engineers and skilled laborers would still not change its actual history. But see how ludicrous one's thinking becomes when the truth is disallowed? The same can be said of this well-ordered world. It is what it is regardless of whether or not one experiences it. It, too, has a specific history that exists outside of our understanding. God created the heavens and the earth, whether God's prized created beings accept or reject that He did. Merely claiming that inanimate factors were responsible for our planet coming into existence does not change its actual history. Whatever arguments one may propose to me to prove that the Great Pyramid of Giza exists, the same opinions may also be put forth to suggest that this world exists the way it does and why. This conclusion is not the result of lofty philosophical calisthenics. Instead, it is common sense that even a child can comprehend. So, an aspiring apologist does not have to begin their journey with apprehension or a lack of confidence. It is quite the contrary. Logic is on their side.

Furthermore, "relative truth" violates the law of noncontradiction. This principle states that opposite ideas cannot both be true at the same time. For instance, either God does exist or He does not, but the conclusion cannot be both. Contradicting statements cannot both be correct; one necessarily must be false.[1]

But it is interesting how devotees of the postmodern worldview tend to pick and choose whenever they conveniently want to apply subjective relativity and when they want to insist upon objective truth. That duplicity is problematic, though, because it is utterly impossible to remain consistent. The search for and the drive to find the truth is ingrained in the psyche of every human being.

For example, *Forbes* magazine, which fancies itself as a relevant periodical for our times, is unapologetic about its postmodern slant on every article that it produces. In March 2019, it published a glowing article about Kylie Jenner. At the age of 21, she reportedly became the world's youngest "self-made" billionaire as the founder of her highly successful cosmetic company.[2] Then, just over a year later, *Forbes* published another article in May 2020 that was not so flattering of the socialite pop star. Evidently, in a desperate bid to rise to higher tiers on the wealth and celebrity earnings list, she had allegedly been forging tax documents and fabricating revenue figures for her company.[3] And the publishers of *Forbes* were very eager to print their corrections. By their admission, "they had spent months uncovering the facts and concluding that their extensively reported investigation was triggered by newly filed documents that revealed glaring discrepancies discovered by their journalists."[4] In another article, they also accused Jenner's family of demonstrating a pattern of "white lies, omissions, and outright fabrications" in their attempt to monetize "famous for being famous."[5]

But in a postmodern world where "your truth is not necessarily my truth," why would the publishers of *Forbes* even care? Why did they spend a handsome sum of money and months of their staff writers' and editors' time digging for the truth about which most of us couldn't care less? What inner moral compass would drive them so determinedly to such ends? And from where did that intuitive sense of right and wrong come? Was not Jenner's truth simply different from *Forbes'* truth? How could they be so politically incorrect as to impose their piety upon such a young victim of privilege? Suffice to say, in a world where it seems that truth does not matter, one would have to guess that it really does, at least when it is wanted.

So, a Christian must not be distracted or intimidated by the rhetoric from the postmodern camp. Its obscurantism is meaningless, and the wise apologist has to see through it, just as apologists have had to diligently confront the false notions of the day in every age since Jesus articulated the truth a couple of millennia ago. Summarily, postmodernism contradicts itself through self-reference; the critique of others by its subscribers would be utterly impossible without the concepts and methods that only reason provides. Therefore, the arguments put forth in the following pages make the most sense even in a new day and age when postmodern thinkers have not quite figured out the integrity of their worldview experiment. So, it is time for Christian defenders of the faith to be "strong and courageous" (Joshua 1:9).

CHAPTER 1
AN OVERVIEW OF APOLOGETICS

KEY SCRIPTURES

1 Peter 3:15-16 If someone asks about your hope as a believer, always be ready to explain it. But do this in a gentle and respectful way.

Jude 3 Dear friends, I had been eagerly planning to write to you about the salvation we all share. But now I find that I must write about something else, urging you to defend the faith that God has entrusted once for all time to His holy people.

Colossians 4:5-6 Live wisely among those who are not believers and make the most of every opportunity. Let your conversation be gracious and attractive so that you will have the right response for everyone.

2 Timothy 2:24-26 A servant of the Lord must not quarrel but must be kind to everyone, be able to teach, and be patient with difficult people. Gently instruct those who oppose the truth. Perhaps God will change those people's hearts, and they will learn the truth. They will come to their senses and escape from the devil's trap. For they have been held captive by him to do whatever he wants.

DEFINITION OF APOLOGETICS

Apologetics means "the rational defense of the Christian faith." As we will see in this chapter, it is the sacred calling of everyone who claims to be a follower of Jesus also to be a defender of the Christian faith, the worldview that He established. The word itself derives from the Greek word *apologia*, which means "a speech in defense" (*apo* (away) + *logia* (speech) = *apologia* (to speak away)).

In the ancient Greek Empire, it was a legal term. Defendants charged with wrongdoing were legally afforded an opportunity to defend themselves with a formal explanation as a part of a fair judicial procedure in court. The accused would attempt to deflect their guilt by "speaking away" the accusations against them and rebutting the charges.[6] Such was the case of the *Apology* by Plato. He was setting forth the case made by Socrates during his trial before the court in Athens.[7]

Similarly, when Christians are charged with believing ideas contrary to secular and religious worldviews, they are called to give a defense for their faith by presenting evidence to substantiate it.

The New Testament was originally written in Greek, and the word *apologia* was employed upon several occasions to describe what the Early Christians had to do to defend their faith in Jesus. For example, in Acts 19:33, idol-makers who were threatened by Paul's effective ministry incited an angry mob to riot in Ephesus. Still, a Jew named Alexander tried to "make a defense before the people." Elsewhere, Paul claimed in Philippians 1:16 that he was "appointed to defend the Good News."

Since opponents whom the Devil was able to convince have always attacked the Gospel, then it has always been necessary to practice apologetics. It is especially true today in a skeptical world that is becoming more hostile to the Gospel. Whether genuine seekers ask honest questions or critics hurl false accusations about the tenets of the Christian faith, Christians must be well-equipped to speak effectively in defense of the Gospel.

The discipline of apologetics is often expressed in a variety of intellectual contexts. Apologists may offer their defense of the Christian faith in relation to scientific, historical, philosophical, ethical, religious, theological, or cultural issues. This book will touch on many of those categories.

Summarily, apologetics provides a *defense* of Christianity as a system, a *vindication* of the Christian worldview against its critics, and a *refutation* of opposing systems or theories.[8] As a defense, apologetics shows that Christianity is reasonable. Its purpose is to show that people have good reason to embrace the Christian faith. As a vindication, apologetics indicates that Christianity is not unreasonable. Its purpose is to show that people do not act irrationally by trusting in Jesus and accepting the Bible as God's Word. And as a refutation, apologetics shows that unbiblical thought is unreasonable. Its purpose is to show that people who reject the Christian belief system act irrationally with any other position they choose to take.[9]

We will examine many of the classical arguments on the following pages, but they are no substitute for faith. Faith is still required to be a follower of Jesus Christ (Hebrews 12:6). However, rational evidence augments, informs, bolsters, and reinvigorates one's faith.[10] Faith in an unseen God, an unrepeatable creation, a divinely inspired book, and One who rose from the dead can be quite a leap for some, but well-established evidence can narrow that gap between what is certain and what is uncertain.

A BIBLICAL MANDATE FOR APOLOGETICS

1 Peter 3:15 is the standard biblical mandate for Christians to be engaged in apologetics. There, the apostle who was considered the first among equals in the Early Church states, "If someone asks about your hope as a believer, always be ready to explain it. But do this in a gentle and respectful way." One should note that with the help of the Holy Spirit (2 Timothy 3:16), Peter instructed believers to make a reasonable defense for what they believe. Followers of Christ are to substantiate the truth claims of Christianity using logical arguments and concrete evidence. Peter gave this mandate for all Christians to give reasons for their faith to everyone who asks, whether those people are earnest, indifferent, or antagonistic.

In the context of verses 13-17, Peter urged believers to be ready to defend their faith even under persecution. He also instructs believers in this passage to possess the proper attitude when engaged in apologetics. Hence, one can be positionally correct, but dispositionally wrong, which will render them ineffective every single time. Pride and condescension will turn people off, but gentleness and respect will go so much further toward earning a right to be heard. Summarily, when the world accuses Christians of being wrong in their worldview, then Christians should be prepared like a defense attorney for an informed rebuttal. They need to be able to build a case for their faith lovingly.

When Jesus commissioned His followers to "go into all the world and preach the Good News to everyone" (Mark 16:15), the reality we face is that many people have objections that hinder them from seriously considering the hope that Jesus offers. This challenge exists because "the god of this world has blinded the minds of those who do not believe" (2 Corinthians 4:4). So, apologetics is about gently resolving those objections so that people will see the truth clearly. Since believers fight spiritual rather than flesh-and-blood enemies (Ephesians 6:12), then their defense is primarily for victims, not opponents. So, unless believers can thoughtfully engage people and lovingly offer rational grounds for considering Christianity, their evangelism and advance of the Gospel will not be nearly as effective.

Similarly, Jude 3 challenges believers to "defend the faith." In English, the word *defend* means to "resist an attack." But in the original Greek language in which Jude wrote, the word *epagonizomai* is best translated "to contend." It means "to struggle against opposition." So, it is absolutely essential that all believers assume the responsibility of not only preparing themselves to give answers to anyone who asks them to give reasons for their hope in eternal life through Jesus, but to also be ready to struggle effectively and resist against evil forces that influence people to oppose and attack the Gospel. It is especially important that Christians hone their skills in the discipline of defending the faith. That objective is what this book is all about—equipping people to be effective at resolving the common objections that people have that are preventing them from seeing the truth.

HISTORY OF APOLOGETICS

After the Church's founding, as recorded in the book of Acts, Christians had to begin defending why they believed what they believed. The history of apologetics can be traced right back to its beginnings in the New Testament. To a puzzled crowd, **Peter** had to defend the supernatural phenomena occurring among the believers (Acts 2:14-41). **Stephen** also had to contend for the life-giving message of Jesus (Acts 7). And **Luke** was a faithful travel companion of the apostle Paul on their missionary journeys. He wrote the most overtly apologetical work in the Bible—his two-volume set called Luke-Acts. Right in his prologue, this capable physician-turned-evangelist stated that he based his work on careful historical research (Luke 1:3). Luke also used the events and speeches of the apostles to present apologetical arguments to a wide variety of audiences.

Paul was highly effective as an early apologist as well. Not only did Luke record and publish many of Paul's speeches (like the one in Athens recorded in Acts 17), but Paul also wrote several letters that were eventually accepted into the canon of Scripture. The entire book of Romans, for example, is a classic piece of apologetics.

In Acts, Paul was tried in court multiple times for proclaiming his hope in Christ. And on each occasion, he had to defend his position compellingly.

> **Acts 22:1** Brothers and esteemed fathers, listen to me as I offer my defense.

> **Acts 24:10** The governor then motioned for Paul to speak. Paul said, "I know, sir, that you have been a judge of Jewish affairs for many years, so I gladly present my defense before you."

> **Acts 25:8** Paul denied the charges. "I am not guilty of any crime against the Jewish laws or the Temple or the Roman government," he said.

Acts 26:2 "I am fortunate, King Agrippa, that you are the one hearing my defense today against all these accusations made by the Jewish leaders."

Furthermore, the beloved disciple and apostle, **John,** also followed a similar strategy that Paul employed. He, too, adopted Greek philosophical and religious terms like "the *logos*" in John 1:1 to challenge his listeners and readers to consider the truth about Jesus. Thus, all Christians should follow the great examples set by the leaders in the first century Church.

Then in the post-apostolic era of the Early Church fathers during the second century, new challenges confronted the Church as the Gospel spread throughout the Roman Empire. Rabbinic Judaism, gnosticism, paganism, and the prevailing Hellenistic culture and philosophy all presented strong opposition to the growing Church and the Gospel's spread. **Justin Martyr** was the foremost apologist at that time. He very successfully used messianic prophecies from the Hebrew Scriptures to prove that Jesus was, in fact, the Messiah. He also refuted common errors and rumors that were circulating widely about Christianity.[11]

In the third century, **Clement of Alexandria** was one of the ones leading the way in apologetics by writing several theological discourses and a more sophisticated and persuasive defense than those who preceded him.[12] But the most prominent apologist of that century was **Origen.** He bravely took on the philosophical, ethical, and historical criticisms of Christianity that existed in his day. His work set a new standard for classical apologetics.[13]

By the fourth and fifth centuries, Latin and Greek apologists became even more systematic in their presentation of the Christian worldview and contrasted with competing secular ideologies. The greatest apologist of this era was **Augustine.** Throughout his life, this gifted writer, thinker, and scholar wrote numerous works that championed Christianity over paganism, refuted heresies, and expounded on truth from a Christian perspective. Known for espousing that faith and reason are merely two sides of the same coin and are interdependent,[14]Augustine also developed the cosmological argument for the existence of God.[15]

Beginning in the seventh century, apologists throughout the Middle Ages directed their efforts toward Judaism, the threat of Islam, and the rational grounds for belief. **Anselm of Canterbury** and **Thomas Aquinas** were two apologists who stood out for their contributions to the defense of faith during this long era. Developing philosophical arguments that became rational proofs to convince atheists, Anselm first developed the ontological argument. On the other hand, Thomas Aquinas took on the resurgence of the Aristotelian worldview that was once again growing in influence.[16] But rather than rejecting Aristotle outright, Aquinas created a Christian philosophy that utilized Aristotelian categories and logic. In doing so, he changed the course of Christian apologetics from that point forward. He is best known for his five arguments for the existence of God.

During the long Middle Ages, there was not much progress in the defense of the Gospel. That is why some refer to that long period as the Dark Ages. But then, in the sixteenth century, the much-needed Reformation occurred, and with it, much more progress in the development and systematic thinking of apologetics. Misguided medieval theologians led to a confusion and perversion of many of the Gospel's fundamental truths. Furthermore, the Renaissance brought further corruption to Christianity due to a preoccupation with pagan antiquity and humanism—a man-centered philosophy that exchanged sin and grace for personal dignity and freedom. But reformers like **Martin Luther, John Calvin, John Knox,** and many others rose to the occasion to protest the errant religious trends of their day.[17] Although they varied in strengths and perspectives, the composite effect of their efforts made a significant impact on the necessary corrections to the essential doctrines of the Christian faith.

During the seventeenth century in Europe, when modern natural science was making breakthroughs and revolutionizing the world, skepticism rose to challenge Christianity. There was a popular notion that faith and reason were incompatible. Thus, apologists had to adapt once again and develop rational responses to the assailants of faith in Jesus. **Blaise Pascal** led the way with an apologetical approach that aimed more for the heart than the head. But he was also persuasive that Christianity is certainly not irrational; it can most definitely be proven true.[18]

Upon the eighteenth century and carrying over into the nineteenth century with the advent of the Enlightenment, Christian apologetics was again forced to adapt to the times and reinvent itself. Secular philosophers like David Hume, Immanuel Kant, and Friedrich Hegel cast doubt on the historical arguments developed by previous apologists. And Charles Darwin also posited a theory that grew rapidly in popularity—a naturalistic explanation for the order and diversity in life that does not require intelligent design.[19] But due to the resistance of these new skeptics, the muscle of apologetics grew even stronger. Today, contemporary apologetics owes a debt of gratitude for the thoughtful responses developed by such outstanding apologists like **William Paley, Thomas Reid, Charles Hodge, Soren Kierkegaard, James Orr,** and a host of others who were not intimidated by the waves of skepticism and criticism aimed toward Christian thought. The teleological argument[20] was added to the cache of apologetical tools along with common-sense realism, an inherent sense of right and wrong, cause-and-effect, and other epistemological theories that are still used quite effectively today.[21]

Then came the twentieth century, and with it, its most famous Christian apologist, **C.S. Lewis.** With such popular arguments as "the trilemma," he insisted that Christianity was based on reasonable evidence and that the true attitude of faith was to believe despite seeming evidence to the contrary.[22] Other twentieth-century apologists upon whose shoulders present-day Christians stand are **Karl Barth, William Lane Craig, John Warwick Montgomery, G.K. Chesterton, J.P. Moreland, Clark Pinnock, Norman Geisler, Francis Schaeffer, Alvin Plantinga, Josh McDowell, Lee Strobel, Peter Kreeft, Hugh Ross, and Ken Ham.**[23] With what seems to be a "shrinking" of the world due to mass communications and affordable transportation, ideas from other world religions crept into Christian thought, bringing a lot of confusion and an attempt to synchronize religions into one. Apologists also had to demonstrate that the Christian faith is the only worldview that can offer coherent and consistent answers to the common questions about the reality of life.

APPLICATION OF APOLOGETICS TODAY

With the advent of postmodernism in the twenty-first century, the idea of rational knowledge upon which most apologetical thought was previously based will need to be updated by an emerging generation of defenders of the Christian faith. Those who tout postmodernism attempt to silence apologists just like all their predecessors did unsuccessfully in previous generations. But it is just a new tactic by the same old opposition. Postmodern opponents of Christianity attack by insisting that traditional apologetical approaches are no longer valid since an increasing number of people reject the conventional canons of logic, rationality, and truth (see the Preface of this book). They insist that we are meant to "share our narrative." Objectivity has been exchanged for subjectivity, universality has been traded for individuality, and absolutes have been swapped out for relativity. This worldview states that truth cannot be defined; therefore, it cannot be used to determine what is real and what is not.[24]

Such a tactic is self-contradictory, though. To insist that "all truth is relative" is to make an absolute statement in and of itself. It does not make any logical sense. This maneuver is nearly as old as humanity itself. We can go back to Genesis 3 in the Garden of Eden and observe the conversation between Eve and the serpent. The serpent asked, "Did God really say..." (Genesis 3:1). In other words, "Is propositional truth really absolute? Can you be certain about what the Creator actually meant? You can be like God yourself. You can redefine what is good and what is evil for yourself." For that reason, apologists need to see this worldview for what it is and not be thwarted by it.

The tenets of postmodernism are an impossibility due to other factors of incoherence as well.[25] For instance, take two bottles out from underneath a kitchen sink. One consists of aspirin; the other consists of rat poisoning. If a person has a headache, then they should believe that the label's text has meaning. Otherwise, the consequences could be lethal. Today, people are not relativistic and pluralistic regarding technology, sports, mathematics, physics, medicine, and just about any other field of discipline. But these views tend to be expressed only regarding ethics. While postmodern advocates will readily admit that the equation 2+2=4 is an indisputable fact, they also only seem to insist upon "your truth" and "my truth" when it comes to their own choices in personal morality. And while people in today's culture assert that everyone has to play by the *same* set of rules in a particular sport, they also claim that everyone gets to play by their *own* set of rules regarding beliefs and behavior. But deviance always has negative consequences. Just as the absence of a standard set of rules in any sport would cripple judgment calls, the absence of a standard set of rules in life would also cripple good judgment as well.

Therefore, postmodern ideology contradicts itself with its lack of coherence and consistency. Its unfounded theories go beyond evidence-based critical thinking and use vague terminology to support obscurant ideas.[26] While on the one hand, it claims that non-Western cultures are out of sphere from Western values and, therefore, should not be judged by our ethical standards, on the other hand, it also champions the cause of women's rights, children's rights, and minority rights, and justly so. Interestingly, stealing, murder, adultery, and child abuse are still considered universally wrong, regardless of the region of the world in which they are committed. But if postmodernism is all about individuals making their own "rules of engagement," then it violates its own rules by insisting that everyone comply with their individualized rulemaking. That kind of circular reasoning is irrational. According to postmodernism, philosophically, anyone can think anything that they wish as long as they do not claim that it is the truth. Morally, anyone can behave any way they want to as long as they do not claim that their way is better. And religiously, anyone can believe anything that they wish as long as it does not include Jesus Christ.[27] See the hypocrisy, tyranny, and tilting of the scales?

At the heart of postmodern ideology is the rejection of the *correspondence theory* of truth. According to this theory, statements are

An Overview Of Apologetics

true when they agree with reality. But once people reject this theory, truth ceases to be defined in accordance with an independent reality. This rationale is permeating our culture today. In search of an alternate theory of truth due to their disillusionment with the age-old correspondence theory, many people embrace the *pragmatic theory* of truth instead. This theory suggests that the ability to produce positive results in a person's life is what determines truth.[28] Although this theory may appear appealing on the surface, it proves debilitated and broken for the reasons stated above. The primary problem for exchanging the correspondence theory with the pragmatic theory is that it moves from a *description* of what is true to a *prescription* for determining truth. But if God is taken out of the equation, then who becomes the ultimate authority for prescribing that new truth? To land upon anyone besides an all-loving God is a perilous alternative.

Therefore, Christians should not succumb to the temptation of tailoring their proclamation of the Gospel to the postmodern culture. It is just a distraction; that is all. The proven arguments are still just as relevant; they may just need to be repackaged, which is what the following chapters attempt to do. Christians must not be deceived in laying aside their most effective weapons—logic and evidence—so that the Church will continue to prevail against the assaults from the god of this world (Matthew 16:18).

As contexts evolve and as Eastern ideologies become more prevalent in a world that seems to be growing smaller and smaller, the defense of Christian thought must expand its diversity of approaches without abandoning the foundations laid in previous generations. Accordingly, to continue fulfilling the biblical mandate of *apologia*, who will pick up the mantle of previous thinkers and strive to make the tenets of the Christian faith relevant today?

CONCLUSION

On a few different occasions, Jesus made promises to His followers that were picked up by Luke:

> **Luke 12:11-12** Don't worry about how to defend yourself or what to say, for the Holy Spirit will teach you at that time what needs to be said.

> **Luke 21:14-15** Don't worry in advance about how to answer the charges against you, for I will give you the right words and such wisdom that none of your opponents will be able to reply or refute you!

What a promise! What an advantage that believers have in their defense of the Christian faith. God, Himself, will help them. The arguments are relatively easy to win. Psalms 14:1 and 53:1 say, "Only fools say in their hearts, 'There is no God.'" In this book, we will see just how foolish it is to believe anything other than the facts of God's existence, His inspiration of a sacred text, His creation of the world, and His plan to come as a Person to reconcile us to Himself.

But every apologist has to remember that people are not just thinkers, they are also feelers. And while an apologist might overcome the thoughts of a critic, if he or she shuts them down emotionally, then that person will not be able to hear at all. And they certainly will not exchange their godless ideas for godly ones, nor will they forsake their wayward lifestyle and embrace one that submits to Christ.[29] It is possible to win an argument, but lose a person, which is never God's intent. God is quite capable of defending Himself; He does not need Christian apologists to help Him. But He does want the lost to be saved by being loved into the Kingdom. Because of this calling, believers must be intent on winning not only minds but also hearts, just as Jesus did.

> **2 Timothy 2:24-26** A servant of the Lord must not quarrel, but must be kind to everyone, be able to teach, and be patient with difficult people. Gently instruct those who oppose the truth.

Perhaps God will change those people's hearts, and they will learn the truth. Then they will come to their senses and escape from the devil's trap. For they have been held captive by him to do whatever he wants.

Effective apologists, then, must also be able to see truth through the eyes of others. Paul quoted Greek philosophers when speaking to Greek philosophers (Acts 17), and he used the Jewish Scriptures when speaking to Jewish people (Acts 13:16–22). He spoke the "language" of those whom he sought to lead to Jesus. Likewise, in a secular culture such as the 21st century, offering secular reasons for spiritual truth is especially strategic. When believers work with the truth that another person has already accepted, then they are more likely to lead them to the One who is Truth.

Christians should commit themselves to seek the Holy Spirit's leading as they endeavor to tackle this book's concepts. They must not forget that human words cannot convert human hearts, convict anyone of sin, or save souls. This work is reserved only for the Holy Spirit (John 16:8–11). He will use His followers in His work of leading people to Jesus, but they must seek His wisdom before they offer their words. This fact is why believers must listen to Jesus before they speak on His behalf. Apologists cannot read the mind and heart of the person they are seeking to reach, but Jesus certainly can. And He knows how best to lead the most ardent dissenters to Himself.

As we begin this journey, will you, as an aspiring apologist, commit to being more interested in the questioner than their questions? Jesus sure is. And we are called to be like Jesus.

A HISTORY OF APOLOGETICS

Century	Apologists	Challenges	Strategies
1st	Paul Peter James John Luke	Jewish Zealots Greek philosophy Roman Paganism and Hedonism	Took what their audience accepted as true and applied Jesus
2nd	Justin Martyr	Rabbinic Judaism Gnosticism Hellenistic mythology and culture Paganism	Messianic prophecies from the Jewish scriptures Refuted common errors and rumors about the Church
3rd	Origen Clement of Alexandria	Roman culture and thought	Challenged philosophical, ethical, and historical criticism
4th-5th	Augustine	European Paganism Heresies in the Church	Fine-tuned a systematic Christian worldview Contrasted to competing secular philosophies The interdependence of faith and reason Cosmological argument for the existence of God
7th-15th	Anselm of Canterbury Thomas Aquinas Martin Luther John Calvin John Knox	Radical Judaism Islam Removal of the Bible from the Laity by the Catholic Church Corruption of Christianity Foundations of Humanism	Rational proofs and philosophical argument Aristotelian logic and Five Arguments for the Existence of God Ontological argument Corrected heresies in the Church
17th	Blaise Pascal	Natural Science Religious skepticism	Aim for the heart, not the head (faith over reason alone)
18th-19th	Thomas Reid Charles Hodge Soren Kirkegaard James Orr	Age of Enlightenment Evolution & Naturalism Humanism Faith is superstitious	Teleological argument Common sense realism Scientific laws to prove the existence of God Epistemological theories
20th	C.S. Lewis Karl Barth William L. Craig Norman Geisler Francis Schaeffer Alvin Plantinga Josh McDowell Lee Strobel Peter Kreeft Ken Ham	Humanism Modernism Skepticism Synchronicity of world religions	Posit reasonable evidences for the claims in the Bible The coherence of Christianity regarding life's questions
21st	?	Postmodernism (truth cannot be known)	Truth is not up for a vote; it exists outside of ourselves

CHAPTER 2

THE ROLE OF FAITH AND BIAS

KEY SCRIPTURES

Hebrews 11:3, 6 By faith we understand that the entire universe was formed at God's command... it is impossible to please God without faith.

2 Corinthians 4:4 The god of this world has blinded the minds of those who don't believe.

Romans 1:18-23 God shows His anger from heaven against all sinful, wicked people who suppress the truth by their wickedness. They know the truth about God because He has made it obvious to them. For ever since the world was created, people have seen the earth and sky. Through everything God made, they can clearly see His invisible qualities—His eternal power and divine nature. So, they have no excuse for not knowing God. Yes, they knew God, but they wouldn't worship Him as God or even give Him thanks. And they began to think up foolish ideas of what God was like. As a result, their minds became dark and confused. Claiming to be wise, they instead became utter fools. And instead of worshiping the glorious, ever-living God, they worshiped idols made to look like mere people and birds and animals and reptiles.

FAITH

When apologists attempt to discuss with others the foundational matters of Christian faith—the existence of God, the deity of Christ, the inspiration of Scripture, and divine origins—strong emotions often get elicited from those who object to such ideas. These feelings range from condescending attitudes to downright hostility. Some people think that faith is beneath the dignity of an informed person. For some reason, believing in something that cannot be proven is somehow an illogical quality of life. The Enlightenment Era of the eighteenth century was known as the Age of Reason—a period when the scientific revolution insisted that everything had to make rational sense.[30] Thus, faith was reduced to superstition[31]—believing in God was on par with believing in Santa Claus, the Easter Bunny, and the Tooth Fairy. Today, as a hangover from that era, there is frequent opposition toward any idea that requires faith, especially in the supernatural. But for those who believe that we should only accept ideas that are proven with absolute empirical evidence, that notion in itself is a belief that cannot be proven. Therefore, that faulty position is essentially self-contradictory.

The reality is that *everybody* has faith. Everybody believes in ideas that they have never proven themselves. Most of the knowledge that we possess has been told to us by others. And we just accepted those ideas as fact without questioning them because we trusted the source.

For example, what is the smallest, complete unit of structure for all substances in our world? Most of us would readily agree that it is the atom. The world's most reputed scientists have suggested this model as the best explanation for universal infrastructure. And it has been put forward without much opposition. How is the atom structured? It is commonly accepted that protons and neutrons are clustered together in the nucleus, and that electrons orbit them.

But how do we know these characteristics about the atom? Has anyone ever personally seen an atom? The reality is that no one had ever seen an atom until very recently with the invention of the Nion Hermes Scanning Transmission Electron Microscope. And still, only a very few people have observed an atom through those powerful lenses; the rest of us just have to believe them. But for decades, though, scientists could merely propose an educated guess. And everyone else believed their propositions in faith.

Now let us probe this thought even further. Even with this widely accepted concept, does anyone know how several powerful, positively charged protons stick to each other so firmly in the nucleus of an atom? Should they not repel each other like two north ends of a magnet? All kinds of ideas about nuclear cohesion have been postulated, but none have ever been proven. The best guess by the most learned scientists is "atomic glue."[32] But no one has ever even seen this hypothetical material. Scientists use the word *hypothesis*, which is just a fancy word for their "best guess."

And why do the orbiting negatively charged electrons not ever collapse into the positively charged nucleus? Are they not attracted strongly to each other? We do not know that reason either. We simply admit that it occurs inexplicably. So, it is evident that we all believe in ideas even though they appear to contradict everything else that we know to be true. Yet we still accept them as fact. These conclusions require faith.

The same is true about the origins of the universe as well. Everyone has ideas that they believe to be true. Some say the Big Bang caused all that we see and experience. Others say that life first came to earth attached to a meteor before it multiplied and spread to become different organisms on this planet. Others say that our universe could have been a product of Intelligent Design, but that we cannot know exactly who or what that entity was. And then others say that God, as described in the Bible, created this universe as a context for human beings to live so that they could be the objects of His infinite love. Yet, these assumptions cannot be proven. People can present arguments for what they believe, but they have no proof to substantiate their claims. So, no matter what one's worldview is, we are all in the same situation; we all have faith. So, the question is not, "*Shall* I believe?" but, "*What* shall I believe?"

Now, since all sides of the common arguments about reality require faith, then we will find that it takes less faith to believe the Bible's claims, and it takes more faith to believe in anything else. Christian theists believe that in the beginning, a transcendent God created everything for a purpose. On the other hand, atheists believe that in the beginning, there was nothing. And something happened to nothing... and then nothing magically exploded for no reason... and then everything came into existence... and a bunch of everything magically rearranged themselves for no reason whatsoever into self-replicating bits... which eventually turned into bacteria... which eventually turned into dinosaurs and other prehistoric beings. It is sad to know that opponents of theism believe such an impossible line of reasoning.

For example, political commentator and Emmy Award winner Ben Stein, who is not a professing Christian, caught up with a few prominent atheists who wield worldwide influence. He asked both of them about their theories of the presence of life in the absence of God. The first person interviewed was Dr. Michael Ruse, a professor of philosophy and biology at several leading universities in England, Canada, and the United States throughout his career. He has also been elected Fellow at two distinguished academic societies. And he founded a journal and authored several books. So, he has quite a pedigree.

The second person was Dr. Richard Dawkins, Britain's best-known academic and the world's most widely publicized atheist. Retired from Oxford University as an esteemed professor, he is also the author of many books that challenge God's existence. And as the recipient of a long list of science prizes and awards, when *Prospect* magazine published a list of the World's Top 100 Intellectuals, they placed Dawkins near the top of the list. In addition to his Ph.D. from Oxford, he has also been awarded eleven other honorary doctorates from some of the world's most prestigious schools. Dr. Dawkins has gone on record, saying, "In order not to believe in evolution, you must either be ignorant, stupid, or insane."[33]

In this interview with Ben Stein about origins, is it possible that these prominent atheists were able to make a closed-case proposition? After all, they are among the smartest people in the world, so they should be difficult to refute. But remember, when one takes

God out of the equation for origins, then they still have to answer how we all got here according to the law of causality. So, what is the next best theory?

In the televised interview, much to Ben Stein's dry-humored shock, they both insisted that the existence of life as we know it is due to "the extra-terrestrial seeding of life forms here on earth." They also suggested that "life arrived here on the backs of crystals."[34] These notions would be absurdly funny if they were not so tragic.

These two distinguished and well-educated atheists were referring to a hypothesis called *panspermia*—an idea that life exists throughout the universe and is distributed among hospitable planets randomly by space dust, meteorites, asteroids, and comets. This theory proposes that microscopic life forms on other planets were trapped in debris and ejected into space following a collision of their host planets. Then those minuscular life forms survived for millions of years somehow before colliding randomly with another planet that possessed ideal survival conditions on its surface. And finally, those micro-organisms became active again and began to colonize their new environment.[35]

Far-fetched? Most definitely. But world-renowned physicist and Cambridge professor, Stephen Hawking, agreed with Dawkins and Ruse. In an Origins Symposium presentation, his notes were taught in absentia, stating, "Life could spread from planet to planet, or from stellar system to stellar system, carried on meteors."[36] Furthermore, Harvard astronomers continue to work on analytical models in a hopeful attempt to make the same suggestion.[37] And three series of astrobiology experiments have also been conducted outside the International Space Station. Astronauts put various biomolecules, micro-organisms, and spores through a battery of tests—all in an eager search to see if the theory of panspermia is plausible.[38] Ironically, a lot of intelligence here on Earth is devoted to proving that no intelligence was required for life to begin here on Earth. But so far, all attempts have been utterly futile (and costly).

This improbable notion begs the question: Is this opinion the best that the best can do? Besides, they still fail to explain where life from the other planets originated; they just relocate the problem elsewhere. And they also fail to provide an idea about how that life would have been able to survive the intense heat that meteors suffer when they enter the earth's atmosphere.

Dr. Dawkins went on to say, "Faith is belief in spite of the lack of evidence."[39] While he meant that statement in a derogatory way about those who believe in God, it is evident that he has succumbed to a considerable amount of faith himself. What takes more faith to believe—a loving God created life here on earth to have an object of His infinite affection, or that meteors brought life here from who-knows-where meaninglessly?

So, there are weaknesses in secularism, atheism, and pluralism. No wonder the late Dr. Antony Flew, the brilliant, outspoken atheist of the twentieth century, finally renounced his allegiance to atheism in his 80s and converted to theism. Having spent a career as a professor at Oxford and debating the students of C.S. Lewis, he eventually insisted that if one just follows the evidence down the path of reason to the very end, then they cannot help but conclude that there is, in fact, a God.[40]

That conclusion was the same one that Lord Kelvin made. The famous 19th-century Scottish physicist said, "If you think strongly enough, then you will be forced by science to believe in God."[41] We will see just how reasonable the existence of God is in a later chapter of this book.

And so many other brilliant scientists have come to that same conclusion as well:

Albert Einstein (a theoretical physicist who famously developed the theory of relativity)—"I want to know how God created this world. I want to know His thoughts."[42] He went on to add, "Religion and science go together. Science without religion is lame and religion without science is blind. They are interdependent and have a common goal—the search for truth. Hence, it is absurd... when scientists say that there is no God. The real scientist has faith... Without religion there is no charity. The soul given to each of us is moved by the same living Spirit that moves the universe."[43]

Louis Pasteur (a French biologist, renowned for his discovery of the process of vaccination)—"Man's first glance at the universe discovers only variety, diversity, and multiplicity of phenomena. Let that glance be illuminated by the science which brings man closer to God."[44]

Johannes Kepler (a German astronomer best known for his laws of planetary motion)—"Those laws [of nature] are within the grasp of the human mind; God wanted us to recognize them by creating us after His own image so that we could share in His own thoughts."[45]

Charles Darwin (an English geologist known for popularizing the theory to evolution)—"The impossibility of conceiving that this grand and wondrous universe, with our conscious selves, arose through chance, seems to me the chief argument for the existence of God."[46]

Galileo Galilei (an Italian astronomer known for his studies in velocity, gravity, relativity, inertia, and motion)—"I do not feel obligated to believe that the same God who has endowed us with senses, reason, and intellect has intended us to forego their use."[47]

Isaac Newton (an English physicist who laid the foundations of classical mechanics)—"He who thinks half-heartedly will not believe in God. But he who really thinks has to believe in God."[48]

Francis Collins (an American geneticist who discovered genes associated with numerous diseases and led the Human Genome Project)—"The God of the Bible is also the God of the genome. God can be found in the cathedral as well as in the laboratory."[49]

Nicolaus Copernicus (a Polish astronomer who formulated a model of the solar system with the sun in the center, rather than the earth)—"The universe was built for us by the best and most orderly Workman of all."[50]

Rene Descartes (a French philosopher who set the standard for modern philosophy)—"I experienced in myself a certain capacity for judging which I have doubtless received from God, like all other things that I possess."[51]

William Carey (a British anthropologist who founded the first degree-awarding university in India)—"Expect great things from God, attempt great things for God."[52]

Robert Boyle (an Irish chemist who founded the inverse proportional relationship between absolute pressure and the volume of gas)—"God would not have made the universe as it is unless He intended for us to understand it."[53]

APPLICATION

For the sake of illustration, let us pretend that the object of our faith is not God for a moment, but rather, the lack of invincibility of a ship. Let us picture ourselves as passengers on a large ocean liner like the *Titanic*. One night, we hear the frantic message from the steward that we have just hit an iceberg, and we are likely going to sink. How does each group respond?

All the atheists on board, who do not believe that the ship is sinkable, do nothing. And the agnostics on the ship, who hope that the engineers' calculations cannot be confirmed, also do nothing. But for all those who believe the steward's message that the ship is going to sink, even though they have been told that the ship is invincible, they run very quickly to the lifeboats and then sort their questions out later.

Now, what if the ship does not sink? Then all the atheists and theists alike end up the same—they go on living. But if the ship does happen to sink, then there is a drastic difference between the fate of the theists and the fate of the atheists. For those who perished due to their lack of belief, sadly it would be too late to change their minds and make the right decision.

This illustration brings us to the proposition of the famous 17th-century French scientist and philosopher, Blaise Pascal. In what he called *The Great Wager*, he said, "Let us weigh the gain and the loss in wagering that God is. Let us consider the two chances. If you gain, gain all; if you lose, you lose nothing. Wager then without hesitation that He is."[54] What does Pascal mean by this profound statement?

Life is fraught with calculated risks. With some risks, though, there is much to gain and little to lose. In those cases, it just makes sense to bet in those kinds of situations. Likewise, it just makes the most sense to "bet" on God, even if we have no proof and no guarantee that He exists.

According to Pascal and many philosophers after him, we do not have the option of not wagering. If we do not wager that God exists, then by default, we wager that He does not exist. Since we are all going to die, and since if God exists, we must answer to Him for our lives, then we automatically wager against Him unless we wager in favor of Him.

If we wager that God exists and happen to be right, then we win everything. Not only do we win a meaningful, purposeful life here on Earth, but we also win eternal happiness in heaven. But if we wager that God exists, and we end up being wrong, then we have lost little, perhaps nothing.

But on the other hand, if we wager that God does not exist and eventually find out that we are right, then we have gained little. In that case, an unbeliever's life is no richer on Earth than the life of a believer. Often, it can be much worse because of the sense of emptiness that accompanies a life void of divine purpose. But if we wager that God does not exist, and we are wrong, then we face eternal separation from God and the associated dreadful consequences of such a damnable condition.

According to this rationale, does it not make sense that the safest position is to wager our lives on the belief that God exists and follow Him in faith? There is everything to gain and nothing to lose if one chooses to believe in God. And there is everything to lose and nothing to gain if one chooses not to believe in Him.

From this chapter, we have seen plenty of information about God to believe if one *wants* to believe. Contrary to the secularists' position, no one has to commit intellectual suicide by believing in God and what He said in His Word. As has been seen by a host of well-known scientists, faith and reason are quite compatible. Faith is simply a rational response to the evidence of God's self-revelation in nature, human history, the Scriptures, and Jesus Christ Himself. Faith is consistent with reason, not contradictory to it. Our beliefs can be grounded in reality, not detached from it. In short, reason tells us that there is a God and that He has revealed the truth. Faith is then a matter of believing what reason has shown God to have revealed. In that sense, faith is not at odds with reason; it is grounded in reason.[55]

There are three different ways to define faith. The first definition is faith despite the evidence to the contrary. It is based on unreasonable beliefs. The second definition is faith without any evidence and is based on beliefs that are blind. The third definition is faith grounded in good evidence. It is based on belief that is attested. The Christian worldview is based on the third definition; God has called His followers to ground their faith in good evidence and then share those reasons with others. This kind of faith is called *forensic* faith—a belief based upon a thorough investigation of all the evidence at hand.[56]

Therefore, the person who believes in God (and all the subsets of Christianity like the Bible, Jesus Christ, creation, etc.) should not be disparaged for having faith. Everyone has faith; even the most ardent atheist has faith. The difference between a Christ-follower and an atheist is that the Christ-follower has faith in *Someone*, while the atheist has faith in *something*. So, faith in Someone is not all that unreasonable. After all, it is undoubtedly better than the alternatives.

One of the earliest apologists, the apostle Paul, said the following convincingly:

> **Romans 1:18-23** God shows His anger from heaven against all sinful, wicked people who suppress the truth by their wickedness. They know the truth about God because He has made it obvious to them. For ever since the world was created, people have seen the earth and sky. Through everything God made, they can clearly see His invisible qualities—His eternal power and divine nature. So, they have no excuse for not knowing God. Yes, they knew God, but they wouldn't worship Him as God or

even give Him thanks. And they began to think up foolish ideas of what God was like. As a result, their minds became dark and confused. Claiming to be wise, they instead became utter fools. And instead of worshiping the glorious, ever-living God, they worshiped idols made to look like mere people and birds and animals and reptiles.

BIAS

Consider an experiment that a professor once conducted in his university classroom. He asked every one of the students to close their eyes. Then with no one peeking, the professor threw a chair up against the wall. Its loud clash created quite a shocking reaction to all the unsuspecting students who did not see that experience coming. At least the professor got their attention!

With their eyes open again, the professor asked all the students to analyze what they had just experienced. Did something extraordinary just happen? They all agreed that they heard a loud noise. However, since they had no absolute proof for what caused it (there were no witnesses because all of their eyes were closed), then the students were left to suggest theories and hypotheses regarding the origin of the noise that they just heard. The professor proceeded:

> How many of you believe that the noise did not happen; it was just everyone's simultaneous imagination?

> How many of you believe that George Washington came back from the dead, threw something that sounded like a chair, and then escaped before anyone saw him?

> How many of you believe that the professor threw the chair lying sideways near the wall in the same vicinity of the noise?

Obviously, the entire class unanimously concluded that the professor was the one responsible for the loud noise caused by the toppled chair being thrown against the wall. Any other conclusion would require far more assumptions.

The classroom experiment demonstrated that people logically make conclusions based on what makes the most sense. Since everyone's eyes were closed, they had to make interpretations of the evidence they had—a noise that sounded like a chair hitting a wall and clanging on the floor, a chair lying sideways on the floor near the wall, and no one but the professor in proximity to that chair. But it was still just an interpretation of all the factors to be considered. Others could dispute those conclusions.

Why were the students so convinced? There is a scientific method made famous by the 14th-century English logician, William of Ockham. It is called *Occam's Razor*. Simply put, it is a principle that many scientists use to choose between two opposing interpretations of the same set of facts. It states that the simplest explanation tends to be the best explanation. And when competing hypotheses are equal in all other respects, then the hypothesis that one should choose is the one that introduces the fewest assumptions while still sufficiently answering the question.[57]

To Ockham's point, when faced with two competing hypotheses about what is observable, an individual is wise to select the one that requires the least assumptions. When the university students had to identify the source of the noise that sounded like a chair hitting the wall—George Washington or the professor—they chose the professor because of his proximity to the chair; it was more likely that he caused the noise. Besides, for George Washington to have thrown the chair, then the students first would have made the following assumptions: that he came back from the dead, found the classroom, timed the noise perfectly to coincide with all the students' closed eyes, and quickly escaped before anyone's eyes could open. Ockham would suggest that because the latter explanation seems unbelievable, then the first explanation should be the one to accept. Of course, this rationale makes the most sense; the students did not need Mr. Ockham to make that deduction when the professor conducted the experiment.

But as we will see in the rest of the chapters of this book, there are numerous competing hypotheses about the fundamental questions of life:

Where did we come from?

Where are we going?

Why are we here?

Is there a God?

Is the Bible reliable?

Was Darwin correct?

Was Jesus more than a carpenter?

And we will see that some claims make a lot of sense while other claims make absolutely no sense at all (or at least they require a much more significant leap of faith). While some conclusions require a lot of assumptions, other conclusions require very little. It is also essential to examine why we see many minds settling for less plausible hypotheses, even if the evidence stands against them.

An individual's worldview is rarely shaped solely by what is proven to be most plausible. Many factors contribute to a predisposed perception of reality. Regarding matters of faith in the traditional sense, there is a considerable amount of confusion about what to believe. On the one hand, the Bible says in Genesis 1:1, "In the beginning, God created the heavens and the earth." Even though there is no proof to back this statement, Christian theists choose to believe this assumption because they accept in faith that the Bible is the ultimate authority for faith and conduct. On the other hand, some agree with the late Carl Sagan, who said, "The Cosmos is all that is, or ever was, or ever will be."[58] While there is no proof for this assumption either, since atheists accept in faith the opinions of secular scientists and philosophers as the ultimate authority for their faith and conduct, then that faith statement is what they choose to believe.

Here we see two conflicting worldviews:

Christian Theists	Atheists and Agnostics
Creation occurred in six days	Evolution occurred over eons of time
In the beginning, God...	In the beginning, the Cosmos...
Humanity came from dust	Humanity came from ape-like creatures

Why are these two views so radically different? Do both sides have the same earth or a different earth? Do theists and atheists have the same fossils or different fossils? Do they have the same physical laws or different physical laws? No, we all have the same set of evidence. Therefore, it is important to note that the disagreement is not about facts because we are all working with the same set of facts. No, the conflict is over the *interpretation* of the facts.[59] And our understanding of the facts is based upon what we believe at the start. It is like we each have different colored lenses in our eyeglasses that tint everything that we observe a certain way. This factor will cause people to disregard one explanation, even though it requires the least amount of faith, and embrace another explanation, even though it requires a much higher degree of faith.

Our presuppositions form our filters and lenses. Regardless of what people are willing to admit, everyone starts with a belief. Everyone has a lens through which they gaze as they evaluate the evidence. Some want to believe that there is a God, so they interpret what they see accordingly. Others do not want to believe that there is a God, so that presupposition affects their interpretations of the same facts.

This approach to facts with presuppositions is called *bias*—a predisposed opinion about something. If we start with a belief in a revelation from God about history, then when we consider the evidence, we will tend to see certain things. But if we start with the belief that God does not exist or have any role in history, then when we consider the same evidence, we will tend to see other things.

Those who claim that this approach is unscientific would have a valid point. But, sad to say, many scientists begin with a conclusion in mind, and then they try to force the evidence to fit that conclusion, even at the expense of falsifying data and hiding facts. As the adage goes, "Never let the facts spoil a good theory."

A classic example of this point is the embryo drawings of Dr. Ernst Haeckel that, until very recently, used to be featured in most public school textbooks. However, his dishonesty was so blatant that he was charged with fraud by five professors and convicted by a university court at Jena. Haeckel's forgeries were subsequently made public with the 1911 publication of *Haeckel's Fraud and Forgeries* by Dr. Joseph Assmuth, Professor of Biology at St. Xavier College.[60] In fact, in his famous book, *On the Origin of Species,* which was published after Haeckel's embarrassing admission, Charles Darwin called the similarity of embryos as drawn by Haeckel "the strongest single class of facts" for evolution.[61] In other words, the father of the theory of evolution deliberately used evidence from debunked science literature that he knew was already known to be false. Incidentally, if the "strongest single class of facts" for evolution has been debunked, then what does this say about the plausibility of the theory of evolution itself?

This unscientific approach is also the case with the hypothetical geological column, the Piltdown Man, the peppered moth, and a host of other "evidence" put forth by determined evolutionists. It is concerning when both integrity and the scientific method can be absent in this all-too-often approach.

Consider this presuppositional bias from Dr. Richard Lewontin, a leading geneticist from Harvard University: "Our willingness to accept scientific claims that are against common sense is the key to an understanding of the real struggle between science and the supernatural. We take the side of science *in spite* of the patent absurdity of some of its constructs, *in spite* of its failure to fulfill many of its extravagant promises, *in spite* of the tolerance of the scientific community for unsubstantiated just-so stories, because we have a prior commitment, a commitment to materialism."[62] In other words, Lewontin said in essence, "I have already got my mind made up; do not bother me with the facts."

Here, he starts with the premise, "There is no God," despite the sound forensic evidence that we will see in a later chapter that suggests the contrary. This well-known scientist admittedly suppresses this evidence while teaching at one of America's most prestigious universities and shaping the minds of an entire generation of high caliber future leaders. All of the facts go through his preconceived lens, and most of them get filtered out. Truth is either ignored or twisted to fit a particular worldview. But this conclusion is not science; it is faith.

These same scientists author the biology textbooks that we find in public schools. And when the question about whether Intelligent Design should be taught alongside Darwin's theory of evolution, The U.S. National Academy of Sciences stated, "creationism, intelligent design, and other claims of supernatural intervention in the origin of life are not science because they are not testable by the methods of science."[63] Bias is seen here since a belief in unnatural intervention in the origin of life cannot be tested by the strict method of science, either.

While scientists who are Christian agree that creation cannot be repeated and presently observed in a lab (the narrow limits of empirical or observable science), they disagree that it is not science (forensic or historical science). However, what those textbook editors fail to admit is that evolution cannot be tested by those same methods of empirical science, either. Evolution cannot be repeated and presently observed in a lab, making it faith, the essence of religion. Here, one faith is merely substituted for another.

CONCLUSION

In the next chapter, all of the evidence that suggests the existence of God will be examined. While there may not be quantifiable, closed-case proof for His existence, this fact does not prove that opponents to God's existence are correct. Both positions must be challenged. Can we prove beyond a shadow of a doubt that God does *not* exist? We do have a reliable source that says He does. And millions of Christians all over the world also testify to His transforming power in their own lives. Hence, the burden of proof is actually upon atheists to refute the claim that God is real. It is no wonder that studies have shown more individuals claim agnosticism rather than atheism.[64]

We are also well aware of the typical arguments. *What about all the evil in the world? What about all the Christians who are hypocrites?* Those questions might be valid complaints, but they are not proofs.[65]

If God does not exist, neither does evil since the absolute standard of morality has been removed. Everything must be considered relative. Therefore, one who does not believe in an absolute standard of morality should be careful not to impose their standards of good and evil upon the rest of humanity.

Furthermore, regarding hypocritical Christians, consider this analogy: Anyone who travels abroad extensively discovers that the main complaint about Americans in other countries is how loud, proud, and self-absorbed some of them can appear to be. But while that observation may be true of a few Americans that they have met, it does not disprove the existence of the United States Constitution or imply that Abraham Lincoln was a mythical figure. Complaints are not the same as proof; they are just diversionary distractions.

Ultimately, there is no solid proof for the atheist position. While Christian theists require faith to believe that there is a God, their faith is not a blind leap. Their position is very plausible. On the other hand, in the next chapter, we will see how the faith of an atheist, void of *any* evidence, requires *more* faith than that of a theist.

Blaise Pascal, the 17th-century scientist/philosopher, said, "People almost invariably arrive at their beliefs, not on the basis of proof, but on the basis of what they find attractive."[66] Similarly, Friedrich Nietzsche, the 18th-century philologist/philosopher, said, "It is our preference that decides against Christianity, not arguments."[67]

Therefore, it is not because people *cannot* accept the truth; it is because they *will not* accept the truth. It is not a matter of the intellect; it is actually a matter of the will.

Canadian theologian James Cantelon, said, "The denial of God has as much to do with our wills as with anything else. To put it simply, belief in God demands responsibility and accountability on our part. It challenges our selfishness. It cramps our style. It demands dependence. And this offends the inner rebel in all of us. Deep down, we truly long for independence. To be free. To be unattached. To call our own shots and do our own thing. To be our own end and beginning—our own God. So, people opt for an atheistic worldview, not because they have thought it through, but because it "frees" them to pursue their own pleasures. If they were honest, they would have to admit that it is a matter of choice; they have chosen to be secularists."[68]

CHAPTER 3

THE EXISTENCE OF GOD

KEY SCRIPTURES

Psalm 14:1 & 53:1 Only fools say in their hearts, "There is no God."

2 Peter 3:5 They deliberately forget that God made the heavens long ago by the word of His command, and He brought the earth out from the water and surrounded it with water.

Romans 1:19-22 They know the truth about God because He has made it obvious to them. For ever since the world was created, people have seen the earth and sky. Through everything God made, they can clearly see His invisible qualities—His eternal power and divine nature. So, they have no excuse for not knowing God. Yes, they knew God, but they would not worship Him as God or even give Him thanks. And they began to think up foolish ideas of what God was like. As a result, their minds became dark and confused. Claiming to be wise, they instead became utter fools.

A LOGICAL APPROACH

Although the existence of the God described in the Bible cannot be proven, neither can His non-existence be proven. But given all the conventional means of logic, we will see that the evidence supporting His existence far surpasses any evidence that would suggest His non-existence.[69] If we were forensic experts, while we cannot see God, we can certainly observe that His fingerprints are truly everywhere. This chapter presents a rational approach to some of the evidence that Christian apologists have at their disposal, thanks to two thousand years of brilliant thinkers who have developed responses to the most vociferous opponents. We will see that the clues to God's existence have a significant amount of force to them.

THE STARTING POINT

In geometry, there is a common practice called the "synthetic approach." It is a method established by the 3rd-century BC Greek mathematician, Euclid. He stated that to prove something to be true, one must first start with what is already known to be true, and then through a series of logical steps, prove what was unknown at first glance.[70]

For instance, consider Pythagoras' Theorem. One may not know the distance of the hypotenuse of a right triangle. However, one may discover the answer to that question since several other factors are known:

1. One side is four units long. (fact)

2. The other side is three units long. (fact)

3. The angle opposite the hypotenuse is a right angle. (fact)

4. Lastly, $a2 + b2 = c2$. (fact)

Given the facts above, a calculation can discover the question's answer, the distance of the hypotenuse. See the illustration below:

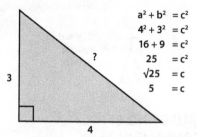

$$a^2 + b^2 = c^2$$
$$4^2 + 3^2 = c^2$$
$$16 + 9 = c^2$$
$$25 = c^2$$
$$\sqrt{25} = c$$
$$5 = c$$

The Pythagorean Theorem

This process of deriving the unknown from the known in geometry is called a *proof*.[71] Applying this principle to apologetics, one must begin with what we already know as facts to arrive at what has yet to be proven. Regarding the argument for God's existence, we must start with what we already know to be true and see if it leads us logically to the answer that we seek.

The best place to start is with oneself. A person knows that they exist. They can be seen, heard, felt, and, from time to time, they can even be smelled. They probably have a birth certificate. They can be measured in height and in weight. They think. They feel. Their actions can be observed. They can love and be loved. They can be experienced. No one can deny a person's existence to them.

You

But how did they get here? Now that a person's existence is indisputable, this perplexing question is crucial. It is one that all God-denying people eventually have to answer. It is this fundamental question upon which the entire balance of science rests. It is why brilliant thinkers like Richard Dawkins, who deny the existence of God, must settle on wild notions such as life being seeded here on a meteor from another galaxy, even though such ideas are fraught with many other unanswerable questions.

THE LAW OF CAUSE AND EFFECT
[THE LAW OF CAUSALITY]

That question, "How did we get here?" brings us to the most certain and universal scientific principle. Martin Heidegger, the influential, 20th-century German philosopher, asked the great philosophical question, "How can there be something rather than nothing?"[72] Intuitively, we resonate with Heidegger's question. To insist something from nothing is to impugn one's credibility. By definition, the basis of all science is the relating of each given phenomenon (an effect) to the combination of factors that produce that phenomenon (a cause), and then describing that relationship in functional form.[73] Everything that exists is contingent; it has a cause outside of itself. The scientific method is the law of causality, relating effects to causes in quantitative equations.[74] A popular application of this law is the children's riddle: "Which came first, the chicken or the egg?" From there, we work our way backward.

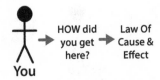

Logically, the Law of Cause and Effect (Causality) inevitably leads us to a choice between two alternatives for how we got here:

1) Infinite Regress—the succession of cause-and-effect can be traced back indefinitely, and nothing is ultimately responsible,[75] or

2) A First Cause—there was a definite beginning point for this chain of cause-and-effect succession to occur.[76] So let us examine and test

the credibility of both of these alternatives and see which one makes the most sense.

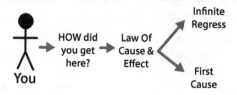

INFINITE REGRESS

During the Age of Enlightenment in the eighteenth century, many scientists who denied the existence of God assumed a theory of an infinite universe. They believed that there was no First Cause. This unsubstantiated notion asserted that the universe had always existed the way it was at that present moment and will continue to exist that way forever. This theory is called *uniformitarianism*—a form of naturalism.[77]

Incidentally, this belief was the popular opinion of the world during Darwin's lifetime. And it provided the crucial element for Darwin's model of origins to appear more acceptable—*time*. In fact, some people refer to time as Darwin's "magic wand."[78] If we could simply go back far enough in time, then some people suppose anything could have happened. George Wald, Harvard biochemist and Nobel Laureate, said it this way: "Time is in fact the hero of the plot. The time with which we have to deal is of the order of two billion years. What we regard as impossible on the basis of human experience is meaningless there. Given so much time, the impossible becomes possible, the possible probable, and the probable virtually certain. One has only to wait; time itself performs the miracles."[79] (It is a comical notion that if a princess kisses a frog and it turns into a prince immediately, then that idea is simply a fairy tale. But if a frog turns into a prince over billions of years, then that idea is somehow considered to be science.)

However, a problem arose with the theory of infinite regress. In 1916, a young but brilliant patent clerk introduced another groundbreaking theory called general relativity, and he refuted such nonsense, albeit reluctantly. Albert Einstein's $E=mc2$ proved that the universe is expanding at an accelerating rate. Edwin Hubble also confirmed this fact in the 1950s with his powerful space telescopes. According to $r=D/t$, when we know the distance that the universe has expanded so far, and we know the rate at which it is expanding, then we merely have to extrapolate backward to find out how long ago the origin of the expansion took place ($t=D/r$). Remarkably, the answer is not billions of years, but rather a timeline that is consistent with the claims of the Bible in Genesis 4-5 (only 6,000-10,000 years).

It is interesting to note that Einstein desperately tried to maintain his atheist worldview at the time. Regarding his theory of relativity, in a letter to Willem de Sitter, he wrote that he was "irritated" with his discovery.[80] In fact, in 1917, he initially published a paper introducing a cosmological constant into the equation,[81] famously referred to as his "fudge factor."[82] This practice forces calculated results retrospectively to match a predetermined outcome (bias). This common approach proves to be unscientific as it shows the observer the desired outcome rather than what the data is showing. Apologists must be astute at recognizing and questioning this irrational method, even when world-renowned scientists practice it.

However, after Einstein's manipulations were exposed in 1922 by a Russian mathematician, the famous scientist confessed that it was "the biggest blunder of his life."[83] Towards the end of his life, though, Albert Einstein admitted, "Science without religion is lame. And religion without science is blind."[84]

Hence, science soundly rejects the theory of infinite regress as it defies logic. Even the most ardent atheists no longer adhere to it. The late Stephen Hawking, the distinguished theoretical physicist, applied mathematician, and probably one of the most brilliant people who ever lived, stated, "Almost everyone now believes that the universe had a beginning."[85]

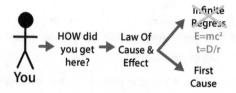

Many other strong pieces of evidence remove the essential ingredient of evolution—eons of time. We can see this evidence in the amount of radiocarbon in diamonds. Carbon-14 cannot remain naturally in a substance for millions of years because it decays relatively rapidly. Scientists from the RATE Project (Radioisotopes and the Age of the Earth) examined diamonds that evolutionists considered billions of years old. But because they discovered significant radiocarbon levels in these diamonds, then their age was shown to be much closer to the age of the Earth as described in the Bible. [86]

The recession of the moon is another prime example of proof for a relatively young earth. The moon's gravitational pull creates a "tidal bulge" on Earth that causes the moon to spiral outwards very slowly. The rate it moves equals approximately 1-1½ inches per year. Because of this effect, the moon would have been closer to the earth in the past. Using gravitational forces and the current rate of recession, scientists can calculate how far the moon has drifted away from the earth over time. If the earth is less than 10,000 years old, then there is no problem because the moon would have only moved approximately 800 feet. However, if most secular astronomy books are correct, then there is a significant problem that people do not take into consideration; a little over a billion years ago, the moon would have been touching the earth's surface.[87]

Human population growth is another crucial evidence to examine when considering the actual age of the Earth. One can approximate the years of human existence after any given point of time by observing how the population doubles every 150 years. A biblical age of the earth (less than 10,000 years) is consistent with the numbers yielded by such a calculation. In contrast, even a very conservative evolutionary age of 50,000 years results in a very staggering, impossibly high figure of 1099, exceeding the number of atoms in the entire universe. An evolutionary timeline does not answer why we do not find such a massive number of people today.[88] So, the current population of just over seven billion people on the planet supports the Biblical claims of the Earth's age.

Scientists often refer to these pieces of evidence as "geological clocks," each supporting the young age of the earth. The evolutionary worldview has to grapple with other significant challenges to its theory, such as the earth's decaying magnetic field, ocean salinity, dinosaur soft tissue, and tightly folded rock strata.[89]Admittedly, there is some evidence that would suggest that the earth is billions of years old rather than thousands, thus providing a greater amount of time for anomalies to occur in Darwin's evolutionary model. Some point to the rock layers in the Grand Canyon and fossils as proof for their theory. However, there are two problems with the apparent evidence for the "old earth" conclusion.

Firstly, one must consider all interpretations of the evidence before them. Instead of dust particles laid down gradually over time to form rock layers suggesting different ages, the same effect could have been caused by rapidly laid sediment during massive water covering. Then as the waters receded, rivers could have carved gorges through the sediment that had not yet hardened. Thus, the rock layers could suggest that a worldwide flood occurred upon a young earth (described in Genesis 6) as easily as gradual accumulation upon an old earth.[90]

Is there any corroborating evidence to support one theory over the other? Yes. Polystrate fossils are petrified tree trunks extending vertically through many horizontal geological strata and can be found worldwide on several continents. [91] This fact means that all of those layers were laid down during the lifetime of an adult tree.

Such an event occurred at Mount St. Helens in Washington in 1980 when a volcanic eruption laid down all around existing trees fresh layers of volcanic debris and pyroclastic deposits. As a result, the South Toutle River cut a deep, new route through the not-yet-hardened layers of volcanic ash, exposing not only many layers of rapidly deposited mud and debris, but also thousands of enveloped trees as well. These trees were vertical and transecting many layers of newly formed Earth.[92] This remarkable observation points to a past geologic cataclysm rather than the steady deposition of sediments insisted upon by uniformitarianism.[93]

Furthermore, fossilized fish, reptiles, and animals also suggest rapid sedimentation rather than a slow deposition. Once an organism dies, it lies in place and decays back to dust. After a few years, no remains are left, not even the bones. But the presence of fossils suggests immediate burial and preservation of the organism by the quick covering of sediment due to a cataclysmic event.[94] Again, Noah's Flood described in Genesis 6 provides a better explanation for the observable evidence than gradual evolution over time.

Secondly, if God created the world in one week according to Genesis 2:1-2 and Exodus 20:11, then He would have had to create a "grown-up" earth.[95] For instance, when Adam was only one day old on Day 7, he would have appeared to be a much older adult. Otherwise, if Adam were only a one-day-old infant, then he would not have been able to sustain life independently. Likewise, everything else would have had the appearance of being much older than they really were for creation to have sustenance.

Suffice to say, the infinite regress theory is implausible for a plethora of reasons.

For more elaboration on why apologists need to contend for a young earth instead of an ideology that includes billions of years, please refer to the author's note at the end of this chapter.

Parenthetically, time is not the only necessary element for Darwin's model of evolution to even seem plausible. The other crucial factor is *chance*. If billions of accidental processes occur over billions of years, then the impossible somehow seems more probable to the advocates of evolution. But just as the time component has been soundly debunked, the chance portion of their argument certainly has been discredited, too.

Consider the simple phrase—"the theory of evolution." The random selection and sequencing of letters and spaces in the correct order by mere chance to arrive at this phrase is a very, very small probability.

Each letter from the alphabet plus one space (totaling 27 possible selections) has one chance in 27 of being selected. And there are twenty letters plus three spaces in the phrase "the theory of evolution." Therefore, chance would spell out this phrase correctly only one in 2723 outcomes, or one success in 8.3 hundred quadrillion quadrillion attempts (8.3 x 1032)! Suppose a machine was used to remove, record, and replace all the letters randomly at the speed of one billion per microsecond (one quadrillion per second). In that case, the probability of this phrase occurring would only be once in 25 billion years by this random method. So, if the earth has been in existence for five billion years, as evolutionists would have us believe, then chance would require five times the amount of time of the earth's entire existence just to spell out "the theory of evolution" at the phenomenal speed stated above. And this simple phrase is infinitely simpler than the DNA code for the smallest life form on this planet.[96]

Furthermore, the scientist/mathematician William Dembski explained that if something happening has a probability of less than 1 in 10150, then it could not have occurred. His number is based on three factors—the number of atoms in the universe (1080), the number of seconds that have passed since the beginning according to evolutionists (1025), and the maximum number of changes that a particle could go through per second (1045). Yet, evolutionists like Julian Huxley suggest that the odds that the horse evolved was one chance in 103,000,000. So, as anyone can see, the odds of evolution occurring by chance is impossible; according to Huxley's numbers (103,000,000 vs. 10150), there is no way that evolution could have happened. The theory violates the law of probability.[97] In fact, the theory of evolution defies all of the established laws of science.

A FIRST CAUSE

Since infinite regress is not a viable option to explain our origin, then the only logical conclusion points to the only other alternative, a First Cause—a definite beginning. And anything with a beginning had to have a Beginner. This argument is also known as the *cosmological argument* for the existence of God.

The First Cause leaves us again with two alternatives for our origins—an impersonal event or a Personal Entity.[98] We find the answer in either a "what" or a "who." The world either came into being by random, inanimate happenstance or by a specific Being with a specific purpose.

All that remains are the two most commonly accepted theories for our origin—The Big Bang (an event) and Intelligent Design (a Person). Let us evaluate the plausibility of both views.

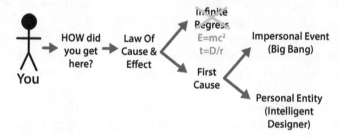

AN IMPERSONAL EVENT—THE BIG BANG

The big bang theory is a relatively young concept in comparison to the entire spectrum of scientific history. It was not until 1948 that George Gamow first offered this theory as a possible solution for the First Cause.[99]

To an eager world audience desperately searching for an explanation for our origins other than God, The Big Bang claims that 13.9 billion years ago, an electric shock struck some primordial material at random, resulting in a cosmic explosion. It does not answer how life appeared from non-life, merely that a series of self-replicating effects that continued to increase in complexity, despite their accidental nature, resulted in the precise order that we see in our world today.[100] Although some sources claim that this theory "is supported by the most comprehensive and accurate explanations from current scientific evidence and observation,"[101] it essentially communicates the notion of "something from nothing."[102]

When one takes God out of the something-from-nothing equation, then what remains becomes very complicated and essentially illogical. (As Psalm 14:1 & 53:1 say, "Only fools say in their hearts, 'There is no God.'") Consequently, the big bang theory has several fatal flaws that render it unsound. However, it still dominates the pages of public school textbooks today. Despite the evidence against this theory, we can observe a clear bias from sources trying to explain a first cause other than God.

First of all, this theory only attempts to explain conditions since the initial "bang." It does not, and cannot, explain the conditions prior to that instance.[103] But this question must be answered. What caused the initial "primordial soup" or the first electrical shock? To assume that these elements were without cause disregards both reason and science. To believe without any hypothesis, especially when it violates the fundamental laws of science, ultimately requires extraordinary faith. The next best alternative must be that life was seeded here by some unknown extra-terrestrial entity like a meteor from another planet. But we have already seen the implausibility of that theory as well.

This faith statement is also profoundly refuted by two other universally accepted laws of science—the First and Second Laws of Thermodynamics. These laws show how things deteriorate from order to disorder, from complexity to simplicity—not the opposite.[104] Living organisms are not evolving; they are devolving. Genetic information is being lost in each successive generation, not added.[105] We know that no new mass and energy is coming into existence anywhere in the universe, and every bit of the original mass and energy still exists, only in different forms.

Furthermore, every time an event occurs, some of that energy is spent and is no longer available. Mass and energy can be changed, but they can neither be created nor destroyed because our universe is a closed system. All phenomena continue to proceed to lower levels of usefulness. So, in the simplest terms, every cause must be at least as great as the effect that it produces. And every cause will produce an effect that is less than itself. Otherwise, there would be a portion of an effect that would be uncaused, which is irrational.

Therefore, if the total amount of mass and energy is limited, and the amount of usable energy is decreasing, then this scientific law is another evidence that opposes an infinite universe.[106] Otherwise, its mass and energy would have been exhausted long ago.

Lastly, if The Big Bang occurred, then all that would remain after the pieces settled would be just that—mere pieces. We can liken the Big Bang to the following scenario: A building where newspapers are printed explodes one day. There was no gas leak and there was no bomb. No one knows why it exploded; it happened inexplicably. Then, as millions of tiny pieces of printed paper fly up into the air, a gust of wind from nowhere just happens to blow all the pieces across the street. Amazingly, as all the newspaper pieces settle, they form a whole newspaper with the next day's news completely accurate.

While the odds of that scenario occurring is infinitely minute, imagine the odds of something as large as the universe exploding, with all the pieces of complexity occurring in such fine-tuned fashion as a result. Now, that notion requires a lot of faith! The idea of design from randomness via chance defies logic.

However, if an Intelligent Designer spoke the universe into existence from a single point, the result would likely resemble an explosion. The only difference is that the pieces would be deliberately placed in order by the Creator on purpose. So, both atheists and theists have the same body of evidence; it is just how each side chooses to interpret the evidence through their predisposed lenses.[107] Therefore, we have to settle on which theory makes the most sense.

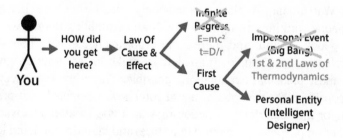

A PERSONAL ENTITY—INTELLIGENT DESIGN

Since science proves the big bang theory to be incredulous, even the most intelligent atheists have pointed to Intelligent Design as the only sound option for its origin. However, in an ardent attempt to leave God out of the equation, the First Cause is often explained as an extra-terrestrial force that "seeded life," which then multiplied and evolved. Even so, a First Cause cannot be explained for those beings, though.

Some have questioned the First Cause of God. Or, "If the universe needs a cause, then why does God not need a cause? And if God does not need a cause, then why should the universe need a cause?" But by the definition of "God," He is eternal and uncreated. Were God to have a beginning, or were He to be a created Being, then He would not, or could not, be God. Since God is eternal, then He is not an effect, nor does He require a cause. He alone, by being the nature of God, is uncaused. Additionally, that which applies inside the closed system of the universe does not necessarily apply to an entity outside of the universe. The argument does not concern a historical figure, but a Supreme Being that exists outside of human limitations and understanding.

The notion that the universe was self-caused proves to be illogical, violating a widely accepted law in logic, the law of contradiction. It states that nothing can create itself because it would need to exist before it came into existence, which is a logical absurdity.[108] Despite the opposition, the evidence supports God as the First Cause.

The Watchmaker Analogy is a beneficial illustration here. Imagine someone walking through the woods and stumbling upon a watch. They look around, and there is no proof available as to how that watch got there. So, they are left to make an assumption given the most plausible explanations possible. There are two theories to consider: 1) Stray bits of metal somehow assembled into precision, or 2) the perfectly functioning watch was created by a watchmaker on purpose, purchased in a store, and later dropped and lost. According to Occam's Razor, which we addressed in the last chapter, conclusions should be based upon the hypothesis that requires the least assumptions. In this scenario, one would wisely conclude that someone merely dropped it. Why? Because the complexity of a watch suggests the existence of a more complex watchmaker.[109] As stated earlier, the cause must always be greater than the effect. The other option is irrational.

Why is it that it is so easy to believe in a watchmaker, but when we study the universe, which is much more complex than a little watch void of consciousness, many people struggle to conclude that there exists a Universe-Maker? If watches cannot evolve from nothingness, then how could complex people evolve from nothingness? Design also suggests intentionality and purpose. This argument is popularly known as the *teleological argument* for the existence of God.

Even Darwin himself questioned the idea of complexity arising from simplicity. In *Origin of Species*, he wrote, "To suppose that the eye, with so many parts all working together, could have been formed by natural selection, seems, I freely confess, absurd in the highest degree."[110]

Nonetheless, he still published these faulty ideas eight years later. The tragic death of his 10-year-old daughter likely contributed to his anger at the idea of God. It is also plausible that publishing these ideas was his way of "shaking his fist at God." Since so many people want to believe that God is not there, they desperately cling to Darwin's theory despite its blatant fallacies, which we will see in a later chapter.

If the complexity and precision of the human eye dumbfounded Charles Darwin, then imagine how amazed he would be with the structure of a single strand of human DNA. Far more complex than a powerful modern computer, all of the human body's information takes up less space than a tiny period at the end of a written sentence. The amount of information in just one strand of DNA is equivalent to a pile of books 500 times higher than the distance from the Earth to the moon, and each strand has different yet specific content. DNA's tremendous order and complexity demonstrate that it had to have been designed by great Intelligence.[111]

According to the commonly accepted Anthropic Principle, for organic life to exist, there are over fifty constants that all have values that together fall into an extremely narrow range. The precision of such constants as the speed of light, gravitational pull, and nuclear forces is so exact that if any one of these constants were off by even one part in a million, then matter would not have been able to coalesce.[112] There would be no galaxy, stars, planets, or people. For that reason, the probability of this perfectly "fine-tuned" calibration happening by chance is so minute that it is considered statistically negligible.

A helpful acronym to help remember the suggestions for an Intelligent Designer is SURGE:

S—*Second Law of Thermodynamics.* Because the universe is continually running out of usable energy, we see that the universe had a beginning because there is still remaining energy.

U—*Universe is Expanding.* Because the Hubble Space Telescope found evidence in the 1950s that the universe is expanding, then we know that it had a beginning and originated from a single point.

R—*Radiation from the Initial Beginning.* When God spoke the world into existence, it would have appeared to have been a "big bang." Creationists believe this beginning had a Personal Cause, while evolutionists believe this beginning had an impersonal cause. However, in 1965, when scientists discovered radiation from this historic moment, it laid to rest any lingering suggestion that the universe is in an eternal, steady state. It had to have had a beginning.

G—*Great Galaxy Seeds.* In 1992, scientists detected ripples in the temperature of the radiation mentioned above. This discovery proved that not only is the universe expanding, but that it was also precisely tweaked to the perfect state. This fine-tuning caused just enough matter to assemble, allowing galaxy formation, but not enough to cause the universe to collapse back on itself. If there had been any slight variation one way or the other, then none of us would be here to tell about it. The project leader who discovered it, Nobel Laureate George Smoot, described them as "machining marks from the creation of the universe" and the "fingerprints of the Maker."[113]

E—*Einstein's Theory of Relativity.* This theory demands an absolute beginning for time, space, and matter. From Einstein's theory, scientists found evidence of the expanding universe, radiation afterglow, and the great galaxy seeds that were precisely tweaked to allow the universe to form into its present state.[114]

CONCLUSION

Some critics object that even if they must accept that an Intelligent Being created the universe, then it still would not singularly prove that this Being is the God of the Bible. This statement is true; however, the clues are very provocative. Since the cause always has to be greater than the effect, and since there can be no effect without a greater cause, then the First Cause must possess all of the following characteristics:

- The First Cause of limitless space must be infinite in extent.
- The First Cause of endless time must be eternal in duration.
- The First Cause of perpetual motion must be omnipotent in power.
- The First Cause of unbounded variety must be omnipresent in phenomena.
- The First Cause of infinite complexity must be omniscient in intelligence.
- The First Cause of consciousness must be personal.
- The First Cause of feeling must be emotional.
- The First Cause of will must be volitional.
- The First Cause of ethics must be completely moral.
- The First Cause of spirituality must be spiritual.
- The First Cause of beauty must be aesthetic.
- The First Cause of justice must be absolutely fair.
- The First Cause of love must be infinitely loving.
- And, most of all... the First Cause of life must be alive.[115]

As one can see, the more one describes the requirements for this world's Intelligent Designer, the closer one gets to the God described in the Bible. With each requirement, His existence makes more sense. Besides, if the God of the Bible was not the Intelligent Designer, then how would the Supreme Being look? This argument is known as the *ontological argument* for the existence of God.

What follows, then, is the *moral argument* for the existence of God. The universal sense of right-and-wrong had to originate from a universally transcendent source.[116] If someone takes the life of someone else, whether it is among the most primitive tribe in the remote jungle of the Amazon or the most sophisticated office towers in Singapore, then it is still considered wrong. This intrinsic ethic exists universally in all cultures and in all generations. And if someone cheats with someone else's spouse, then it, too, is considered wrong in all cultures and all generations. Furthermore, if someone steals someone else's property, then it is also regarded as wrong in all cultures and generations. But where did this timeless, worldwide sense of right and wrong originate? Universal morality requires a transcendent moral Lawgiver.

Regarding the well-known problem of the chicken and the egg mentioned earlier, we have an answer for which came first. God created that first chicken with a plan and purpose to kick-start the procreation process. See? When God is allowed to be a part of the solution, then the riddles of life are much easier to decipher.

A great question to ask those who challenge the idea of God as the Intelligent Designer and the adequate First Cause is, "Were you there?"[117] Because no one was there, then no one can insist with absolute certainty that their view is correct and that the Christian view is incorrect. But actually, Someone was there. And He told us all about it in His Word. It would behoove us to listen to this Eyewitness and consider what He has to say.

Francis Collins, Director of the Human Genome Project, led a team of over 2,000 scientists who collaborated to determine the three billion letters in the human genome—our DNA instruction book. He concluded, "I cannot see how nature could have created itself. Only a supernatural force that is outside of space and time could have done that."[118]

Francis Schaeffer, world-renowned 20th-century philosopher, stated, "Beginning with the impersonal, everything, including man, must be explained in terms of the impersonal plus time plus chance. Do not let anyone divert your mind at this point. There are no other factors in the formula, because there are no other factors that exist... No one has ever demonstrated how time plus chance, beginning with an impersonal, can produce the needed complexity for the universe, let alone the personality of man."[119]

So, Christians can be confident that what the Bible says about the existence of God is true. They can likewise be confident that any other theory for our origin lacks credibility and sound evidence.

Author's note about the importance of the young earth and the seven literal 24-hour days of creation:

Why take so much space here in this chapter about the existence of God to address the crucial time element for evolution? Why labor this point by emphasizing the 6000-year age of the earth according to the seven days of creation in Genesis 1 and the subsequent genealogies in Genesis 5-11? Why is it utterly impossible to try to fit billions of years into the creation week by attempting to redefine the word *day* in Genesis 1 from a literal 24-hour period to something else? *Because it is a crucial theological issue.*

First of all, the idea of billions of years came out of the secular belief that fossils were laid down before people ever existed. But the Bible makes it very clear that death came after the first people sinned—not just death, but also disease, suffering, and evil. In the fossil record, we not only have a long history of death, but we also have evidence of diseases like cancer and arthritis as well as indications of violence between animals. But the Bible says in Genesis 1:31 that when God looked upon what He had created, He declared that it was all "very good." However, God could not have looked upon death, disease, suffering, and evil and call it very good; it is inconsistent with His divine character. Therefore, all of these ill-effects had to have come *after* people introduced sin into the world and the world became cursed (1 Corinthians 15:21a). Otherwise, people could blame God for all that is bad in the world. God created this world very good; but people's sin afterward had severe consequences.[120]

The second theological issue is the need for a Savior. Why did Jesus come to earth in the first place? He came to pay the penalty of our sin, which is death (1 Corinthians 15:21b). But if death existed before sin, then why did Jesus have to come? See? The notion of billions of years drains the Gospel of its effectiveness. It not only blames God rather than people's sin for death, disease, and suffering, but it also removes the need for Jesus.[121]

There is also a third problem with carelessly redefining Genesis 1 to reconcile with ungodly ideology. Suppose people are told that the

Genesis 1 account cannot be taken literally. In this case, it will not be long before this idea is applied to other areas of the Bible as well, compromising the entire authority of Scripture. If one cannot trust Genesis, then how can they trust the rest of the Bible? We simply cannot take the ideas of fallen humankind and reinterpret Scripture. Otherwise, we are exalting people's ideas above God's ideas. The gap theory, day-age theory, and theistic evolution are all faulty ideas, and they simply do not work when seriously examined.

Lastly, Genesis 1-11 establishes all of the central doctrines of the Bible, and the truth regarding the controversial issues of today—abortion, marriage, gender, sexuality, and race—are also addressed in these chapters. If the account of Genesis is either dismissed or reduced to an allegory and declared that it does not matter, then we remove the authority of Scripture on all the doctrines and current issues that the Church is commissioned to address in the twenty-first century.[122]

An apologist needs to be prepared to defend biblical truth even when presented with Christian misinformation. Why is it that a "day" describes a literal day everywhere else in Scripture except Genesis 1? Why is it that no one disputes that Joshua led his army to march around Jericho for seven days, not seven million years? Why is it that no one suggests that Jonah was in the belly of a fish for three million years, not just three days? When people read the word "day," which was the Hebrew word, *yom*, they always interpret it as a literal, 24-hour day... except when it comes to Genesis 1. For some reason, people feel compelled to change the meaning of the word "day" to mean millions of years. Why is that? Because they attempt to take an anti-God rationale, an ideology designed to remove God out of the equation and force it to fit into the biblical account. But in doing so, they jeopardize the power of the Gospel because they inadvertently blame God for evil, remove the need for a Savior, and undermine the authority of Scripture. So, apologists have to defend the literal interpretation of Genesis 1; there were indeed seven, 24-hour days of creation. Period.

Why do Christians doubt that God, who is all-wise and all-powerful, could have created the whole universe in six literal days and rest on the seventh day? Why try to make creation fit into a naturalistic ideology? Why could God not create a grown-up earth instantly? This struggle exists because our world is deeply influenced by a culture shaped by a secular worldview. And many find themselves attempting to reconcile the two views to appease critics and skeptics. But it is not necessary. Actually, it is impossible.

In summary, one cannot take the world's atheistic ideas and try to add them to the Bible. Such syncretism was frowned upon sternly in the Bible when the Samaritans tried to accommodate the world's religions and blend them with the Holy Scriptures. Similarly, evolution is a pagan religion that tries to explain the presence of life without God. Sadly, Christians often take this ungodly view and try to add it to the Bible, attempting to synchronize the Genesis 1 Creation Week with evolution. From a theological standpoint, this practice is very dangerous.

Martin Luther, the great 16th-century Reformer, summed it up well when he stated, "If you cannot understand how creation could have been done in six days, then grant the Holy Spirit the honor of being more learned than you are."[123]

CHAPTER 4

THE RELIABILITY AND INSPIRATION OF THE BIBLE

KEY SCRIPTURES

2 Timothy 3:16 All Scripture is inspired by God and is useful to teach us what is true and to make us realize what is wrong in our lives. It corrects us when we are wrong and teaches us to do what is right.

1 Thessalonians 2:13 We never stop thanking God that when you received His message from us, you didn't think of our words as mere human ideas. You accepted what we said as the very word of God—which, of course, it is. And this word continues to work in you who believe.

2 Peter 1:20-21 Above all, you must realize that no prophecy in Scripture ever came from the prophet's own understanding or from human initiative. No, those prophets were moved by the Holy Spirit, and they spoke from God.

Psalm 119:160 The very essence of Your words is truth; all Your just regulations will stand forever.

THE BIBLE AS A RELIABLE HISTORICAL DOCUMENT

If a historical document makes a claim, then those who doubt its claim have the responsibility to refute it. In other words, when the Bible stands on trial, then to be fair, it should be considered innocent until proven guilty. The burden of proof for one's position about the Bible should not be upon Christ-followers, but rather upon its critics. But since critics rarely play by those well-established rules of literature, then to equip the apologist, we should consider the following ideas.

What does the Bible say about itself? All Scripture, every single verse, is divinely inspired (2 Timothy 3:16). Therefore, we cannot be selective with which parts of the Bible we wish to believe and which parts we wish to reject. All of it, in its entirety, is useful to us. God superintended the writers of Scripture to write what He wanted to be expressed, and He kept them from error in doing so (1 Peter 1:20-21). Therefore, since the Bible is the revelation of God to humankind, then it must be our fixed source of authority for faith and conduct (1 Thessalonians 2:13). Without error, it is absolutely sufficient, and it is endurable for all generations and cultures.

In the previous chapter, we saw that it is quite conceivable that one transcendent God exists—one who is both knowable and approachable. So, if He desired to communicate to His prized creation, not only that He exists, but also the terms by which He could be known, then how would such a correspondence look? Given His moral purity and our moral depravity, what necessary message would it need to say? Could God move upon various people to write what He wanted them to say and then compile it all in a book? Why not? He is God. In this chapter, we will see that the Bible is the most logical explanation for God's communication with people. We must address this issue. With such an enormous historical presence, the Bible has been the dominant piece of literature and prevailing influence upon history and culture for the past 2000 years. It simply cannot be ignored. No other single piece of literature has ever come close to its reach and impact upon entire civilizations. Let us first examine how it stands against other prominent literary texts.

Who wrote the *Iliad*? Most of us were informed in grade school, without hesitation, that the author of *Iliad* was Homer, a Greek epic poet who lived around the twelfth century BC. Second question: Do historians use this book as a basis for their understanding of the events that occurred during that particular era? The answer is *yes*. The historical events recorded in this book are understood and taught as facts in public schools. So, let us examine this story.

Briefly, the *Iliad* is the account of the final year of the Trojan War, which was a ten-year siege against the King of Ilium by a coalition of Greek states led by the legendary warrior, Achilles, for his king, Agamemnon. As the story unfolds, it tells of human warriors inter-acting with Olympic deities such as Zeus, Athena, Apollo, Aphro-dite, and Poseidon. These gods and goddesses end up fighting and destroying each other as humans become caught in the fray. It is almost as if supernatural forces rather than military strategists determined the fate of these warring cities in that day.[124]

Although the story is wrought with Greek mythology and mystical events, literary scholars and historians attempt to distinguish between the battles among people and the battles among the imag-inary gods. They then embrace the battles among the people as truth, and they dismiss the fighting among the gods as fiction.

But where does one draw the line between fantasy and reality? If the god Apollo did not exist, then how do we know that the human warrior Achilles did? The text records both as real entities with which to be reckoned. And how do we know that Homer was the actual author? The authorship is disputed among literary analysts.

Even more concerning is that the work claims to have been written in the 900s BC, 300 years after the events described by Homer in his book, and the earliest available partial copy of the *Iliad* is dated in the 400s BC. So, there is a 500-year gap between the original and the earliest partial copies—and not many of those extant copies are available for comparison.[125] That span is a great deal of time, not only between the event and the recording, but also considering the copying and re-copying by hand in the absence of a printing press. The earliest available complete copy of Homer's *Iliad* actually suffers a 2200-year gap from the original.

Furthermore, due to a high illiteracy rate at that time, we know that the storyline was passed down by oral tradition from generation to generation during most of that time gap. Anyone can attest that facts can become very distorted when an account is told and re-told again and again. No doubt, there were imaginative embellishments and deletions in the plot along the way so that the story became more of a legend than a recording of factual events. There is no wonder that of the 15,600 lines of script, there are 764 variations—equating to 5% of what literary scholars call "textual corruption."[126]

Additionally, there are no other contemporary authors who corroborated Homer's account. And though archeological discoveries make it possible that the story is loosely based on a real conflict, its nature and length are thought to be completely different. Countless errors contradict the culture of that time. Historian Moses Finley famously asserted that it's "catalog of errors is very long." [127] Though historians admit that there may be some historical basis, it is agreed that the events of the *Iliad* cannot be entirely relied upon as a historical account.[128] It is also a known fact that Homer's works were not written so much for historical purposes as much as they were for entertainment purposes (poems and playwrights).[129] So, his emphasis was not on accuracy. Imagine a digital file of *Forrest Gump* being locked in a time capsule and discovered 1000 years from now. What if the people then were to use it as a basis for historical fact to describe the latter half of the twentieth century?

Despite all the above problems, there are still only a few that question the *Iliad*'s historical reliability. Why? Because we approach the *Iliad* like we do all other ancient documents—"as is" until proven otherwise.

The first rule of thumb in determining the authenticity and reliability of ancient documents is called Aristotle's Dictum. It states that only inaccuracies can lead to a rejection, never the other way around. We should always accept the claims that a document makes of itself unless there is reasonable question otherwise due to inner contradictions and outer factual inaccuracies.[130] When any piece of literature is under investigation, whether it is secular or sacred, it is always given the benefit of the doubt. The burden of proof is always upon the skeptic. To assume fraud before analysis is considered unacceptable in any branch of science, including the analysis of historical documents. Lastly, difficulties and unanswered questions do not constitute a rejection. They only indicate that further investigation is required.

Rules for determining historical authenticity of ancient manuscripts like the *Iliad* have been well established and have been widely accepted for centuries. It is what scholars commonly refer to as "textual criticism."

However, when examining the Bible's reliability, critics tend to change all the rules and place the Bible unfairly in a category all by itself.[131] Instead of inaccuracies leading to rejection, prior rejection leads to an all-out attempt to prove possible inaccuracies. And instead of the burden of proof being placed upon the critics to demonstrate the Bible's lack of reliability, quite the opposite is true—Christians are regularly required to prove that the Bible is true. But for the sake of adding a foundation to the Christian faith and gently providing a rational answer for the hope that followers of Christ possess, we will continue with a logical analysis anyway.

Since the Bible is a historical document, a fact that cannot be denied, then let us examine its reliability with the same criteria by which all other historical documents are analyzed. Let us apply the methods used in a discipline called *historiography*—the science of testing the reliability of ancient manuscripts.

Three common tests are used in any evaluation:

1. Bibliographical test

2. Internal evidence

3. External evidence[132]

1. BIBLIOGRAPHICAL TEST

This test is the examination of the textual transmission by which documents have reached us. Most ancient documents were written on material that disintegrated over time. So, in the absence of an original copy, the measure of its reliability is determined by:

- Number of early, extant copies (for comparisons)
- Time interval between the original and available copies
- Textual variation between those copies[133]

The *Iliad* was referenced earlier because it is considered the most reliable work in ancient literature, boasting a textual corruption of only 5%. As was pointed out, there remain major questions, but these questions have not led to its rejection. We simply accept the claims that it makes about itself until we see absolute proof otherwise.

But the Bible's historical reliability is far greater than that of the *Iliad*. Let us compare.

Iliad	Bible
Written: 900+ BC	Finished writing: 100 AD
Earliest extant copy: 400+ BC	Earliest extant copy: 125 AD
Gap: 500 years	Gap: 25 years
Number of early copies: 640	Number of early copies: 24,633
Textual variation: 764/15,600 lines	Textual variation: 40/20,000 in N.T. (only 400 words, none of which change the meaning (ie: spelling differences)
Textual corruption: 5%	Textual corruption: 0.5%

For the Bible, there is only a gap of 25 years between when some of Paul's latest pastoral letters and John's Revelation were written and their earliest extant copies. Sir Frederic Kenyon, former Director of the British Museum and considered one of the greatest literary scholars of all time, said that this interval is so small that it is deemed to be negligible. Therefore, the authenticity of the Bible may be regarded as established.[134]

The Bible is a more accurate reflection of what was initially written than any ten pieces of classical literature combined. For instance, there are only seven copies of Plato's work, and the gap between the lost original and the earliest copied manuscript is 1300 years. Another example is found in Caesar's *Gaelic Wars*. Though only ten copies remain, with a gap of 1000 years, reputable historians consider both of these works accurate and reliable according to standard principles of historiography.[135]

Furthermore, the Bible is in much better textual shape than any of the 37 plays written by William Shakespeare. This point is astounding, considering that Shakespeare wrote his plays in the seventeenth century, which was over 200 years after the invention of the printing press.[136] Yet, there are gaps in the text in every one of his plays where the publisher is left to speculate what he originally intended. This problem forces scholars, then, to make educated guesses to fill in the blanks. However, they are not all in agreement. Most of us never had that important piece of information in our high school literature classes. Yet, regarding the transmission of the text of the Bible, through bibliographical tests, it is remarkable that absolutely nothing has been lost over time.

2. INTERNAL EVIDENCE

A document's consistency, or lack thereof, is another excellent indicator of its authenticity.[137] If a document contradicts itself, then there exists a reason to question its veracity. By continuing to employ the historiography rules of literary research, let us measure the Bible's reliability by its internal evidence.

The Bible was written over 1,500 years by at least 40 different authors from every walk of life—kings, peasants, philosophers, fishermen, politicians, military officials, doctors, and rabbis. It was also written in many different places—the wilderness, a dungeon, a palace, on the road, on an island, and elsewhere. Its pages came from 13 countries on three different continents and was written in three different languages—Hebrew, Greek, and Aramaic. On top of all that wide diversity, its contents include hundreds of controversial subjects such as ethics, family roles, and doctrine. But even though the contributors of the Bible are so diversified geographically, economically, historically, culturally, and educationally, there is still only one theme from cover to cover—God's redemption of humankind through Jesus Christ. And there is still only one consistent moral standard. Also, there are absolutely no contradictions.[138]

To recognize the magnitude of this incredible fact, consider a gathering of 40 college students in a classroom today. Propose a question about just one moral subject. In this postmodern culture, it would be impossible to get a unanimous answer. There would be a significant lack of continuity despite similarities in all the students' location, age, language, relative economic class, school system, and culture.

Thus, in light of the overwhelming consistency of the Bible, despite the wide range of diversity from its contributors, one would be tempted to suspect that the Bible is the work of just one Author instead of forty. We will consider the concept of divine inspiration in the second half of this chapter. But suffice to say, for now, the Bible is incredibly consistent.

3. EXTERNAL EVIDENCE

This category of historical tests assesses whether other historical materials outside of the document in question either confirm or deny the claims made by the document itself.[139] Investigators consider supporting evidence offered by other authors who were contemporary to the time of the document's writing. They also consider evidence from archeology. Are the claims in the document consistent with other discoveries?

Again, the Bible wins "hands down" over any other literary piece of antiquity. In fact, many historical events that are regarded as firmly established have far less documentary evidence than many biblical events. For example, there is significantly more historical support for what Jesus said and did than there are for the exploits of Alexander the Great.[140] In fact, the first records about that ancient Greek king appear 400 years after his death. In contrast, the first records about Jesus appear less than a decade after His ministry on earth—not only by eyewitness followers, but also by secular historians as well.

There are over 36,000 quotations from the Bible by people either living during the time of a particular biblical portion's writing or by those living right after the canon of Scripture closed.[141] There are also thousands of references to the people and events mentioned in the Bible by contemporaries of those named. The following people are just a few familiar examples of historical repute: Josephus, Ignatius, Polycarp, Clement, Papias, Origen, Tertullian, Cyprian, and Justin Martyr.[142]

Furthermore, for centuries, critics degraded the Bible as legendary and fictitious for lack of archeological proof for many of its references—even though the methods and effectiveness of modern archeology are only about 175 years old. It stands to reason that, just as the general body of knowledge is increasing rapidly in the world, so, too, is archeological knowledge. Presently, over 25,000 sites show some connection to the Old Testament period of the Bible. And in every single case, the biblical record has been affirmed even further.[143] For example, the discovered ruins of Jericho's walls show that they did in fact collapse intact—something that has never happened again, yet it is recorded in the Bible (Joshua 6:20). No wonder that after spending a career on the field, noted archeologist Nelson Glueck declared, "It may be stated categorically that no archeological discovery has ever controverted a biblical reference."[144] Rather, archeological facts fortify most historical accounts of the Bible. So, at this point, any criticism of the Bible's historical reliability remains from a period when a lack of knowledge led to premature criticism.

CONCLUSION OF BIBLICAL RELIABILITY

The most obvious and straightforward question that critics and skeptics of the Bible must answer is this: Can one prove that any part of the Bible is false by showing that it either contradicts itself or disagrees with a known fact that exists outside of itself? The climate has grown conspicuously silent as we await an answer. Renowned scientific scholar, Henry Morris, claimed, "If Christianity is false, then the existence of a fallacy of such scope as the Bible constitutes a greater miracle than if it were true."[145] In other words, in light of the overwhelming satisfaction of the strict rules of ancient document analysis, it takes more faith to believe that the Bible is a fraud than to believe that the Bible is an accurate, reliable, trustworthy, historical document.

After diligently attempting to disprove the Bible, former atheist Josh McDowell stated, "After personally trying, as a skeptic myself, to shatter the historicity and validity of the Scriptures, I had to conclude that they actually are historically trustworthy. If a person discards the Bible as unreliable in this sense, then he or she must discard almost all literature of antiquity."[146]

Another professor wrote, "If you are an intelligent person, then you will read the one book that has drawn more attention than any other, if you are searching for truth."[147]

It is interesting to observe that when we place the Bible beside the next best reliable ancient manuscript, the *Iliad*, complete with all the *Iliad*'s inaccuracies, unverified positions, and references to mythological gods as facts, one is rejected while the other is accepted. Why is that? Truth be known, most critics of the Bible have never even opened it, much less ever read it and conducted an honest appraisal of its reliability. So, we must understand that the Bible is not rejected due to inaccuracies like any other historical document would be. There are no mistakes or contradictions within itself or with any historical events and scientific facts.

People reject the Bible simply because of what it says—the claim that we need to submit our will to God's will.[148] The cursory overview of the evidence explored in this chapter is more than sufficient to convince any honest scholar. But as we have seen in previous chapters, the problem of unbelief is not due to the intellect; it is due to the will. People are not *unable* to accept the Word as Truth; they are simply *unwilling*. To acknowledge the Bible's authenticity is to be confronted by what it says about humanity's condition. Living in denial is the all-too-familiar way that many people deal with conviction. But this wager is quite risky considering that all of eternity is at stake.

Now that we have made a case for the Bible's reliability, the next portion of this chapter will examine the Bible's divine inspiration. Since we can trust the Bible to be accurate under the most intense investigation regarding historical and scientific matters, then it is also reasonable to trust it in the search for spiritual truth.

THE BIBLE AS A DIVINE SOURCE OF INSPIRATION

Try to solve the following puzzle:

Wh n n rb tr r ly t k s t ll th v w ls n p r gr ph, th n ts m ss g b c m s v ry d ff c lt t d c ph r. B t wh n v w ls r ll w d t b ncl d d, th n v ryth ng f lls nt pl c nd th m ss g m k s p rf ct s ns.

We will explore the answer to this puzzle later in this chapter and why this exercise is relevant.

Given the evidence, both internally and externally, and the superior bibliographical information discussed in the first portion of this chapter, the Bible's authenticity can certainly be considered established. Then, once a document's authenticity is proven, the next logical conclusion is to accept what it claims as truth. Abiding by that understandable and acceptable rule of historiography, the Bible claims divine inspiration over 2600 times in just the Old Testament alone.[149] Therefore, its authenticity and reliability validate its claim of divine authorship.

What does divine inspiration mean? It does not mean some type of "mechanical writing" where the writers surrendered control to some spiritual force. It cannot be confused with the entertainment industry's portrayal of occult practices. Divine inspiration also does not equate to dictation, whereby God spoke audibly, and the writers just acted as His secretary. Rather, divine inspiration means that God used each personality as instruments and guided them so that they wrote what He intended.[150] Therefore, Isaiah is different in style than Jeremiah, just as Matthew and John's styles are different. In fact, the four gospels reflect the four different primary personality types of people.[151]

Some skeptics still insist upon their doubts despite their lack of evidence to support their rejection of the obvious. To insist, though, that the Bible is not authentic (thus, uninspired) necessarily means to charge the writers with fraud. How does that claim hold up under investigation? The following considerations of the New Testament authors alone seriously discredit that notion. (It is important to note that once we validate their authorship, this evidence automatically validates the Old Testament authors since the New Testament authors fully endorsed them.)

INVESTIGATION OF BIBLICAL AUTHORSHIP

The fabrication of such a theme would point to a conspiracy involving a large number of people with such diversity that collaboration would be almost impossible.[152] At least eight authors and many more associates wrote the New Testament letters at widely scattered times and places.

Evidence of collusion is also totally absent in the writings themselves. Each writer offers his perspective as he gives his independent witness.[153] While not contradictory, their accounts are different but complementary, much like the old Indian parable of several blind men attempting to describe what they feel as they touch different parts of an elephant for the first time.[154] While one insists that the elephant is hard and narrow (the one feeling the tusk), another insists that the elephant is soft and wide (the one feeling the belly).

Furthermore, the information recorded is not about generalities and private events in the lives of the authors. Rather, the biblical record has countless references to public events, places, and people that are verified by other sources outside of the New Testament.[155]

Another point to consider is the absence of fraud and hypocrisy in the Bible, especially since such sins are seriously forbidden. Instead, the writers write with incredible conviction. And the fact that most of the writers were willing to be martyred for their convictions is the crowning proof, not only of their sincerity, but also the legitimacy of their claims. There would have been no incentive to fabricate their accounts.

One might ask, "What if they were sincere, but sincerely wrong (as followers of cult groups are often known to be)?" Cult members can be convinced, but mistaken, as subjects of mass delusion or hysteria. However, the New Testament writers reported events that took place publicly among crowds of people, not in isolated, dark corners or compounds. The events also included various times and places by many people of varied backgrounds—unlike all other documented cases of mass delusion. Those who recorded the biblical accounts do not fit the profile of individuals prone to hallucinations and lacking in credibility—people such as Paul (the best educated), Luke (a competent physician), Matthew (a well-known federal employee), and James (a prominent leader of the Early Church). Lastly, what they recorded was accepted by significant numbers of people at that time despite severe persecution that would have forced them to analyze the writers' claims carefully.[156]

The fact that the writers of the Bible were people of credibility and their subject was accepted by great numbers of people at the time is a strong indicator that the claims of the Bible are true, including its divine authorship.

FULFILLED PROPHECIES

Perhaps the most significant indicator of divine authorship is found in the number of fulfilled prophecies throughout the text. This feature also makes the Bible unique among all other sacred religious writings. There are hundreds of examples of prophecy, or history being written in advance with absolute accuracy. This phenomenon is something only the one true God could do, One who exists outside of the time/space continuum.[157]

One great example is the sequence of empires described in detail in advance in Daniel 2—Babylonian, Medo-Persian, Greek, and Roman in succession. Another is the number of prophecies about cities that would rise and fall—Tyre (Ezekiel 26:4-5), Babylon (Jeremiah 51:58), and Edom (Obadiah 18). But perhaps the most remarkable example of fulfilled prophecy is related to the life and ministry of Jesus. There are well over 350 Old Testament prophecies fulfilled by Jesus, as recorded in the Gospels.[158] The following are just a few examples:

1. He would be born in Bethlehem
   (Micah 5:2 > Matthew 2:1)

2. He would be preceded by a messenger
   (Isaiah 40:3 > Matthew 3:1)

3. He would be betrayed for thirty pieces of silver
   (Zechariah 11:12 > Matthew 26:15)

4. The betrayal money would be used a certain way
   (Zechariah 11:13 > Matthew 27:7)

5. He would be silent before His accusers
   (Isaiah 53:7 > Matthew 27:11-14)

6. His hands and feet would be pierced
   (Psalm 22:16 > Matthew 27:35)

7. He would be given gall and vinegar to drink
   (Psalm 69:21 > Matthew 27:34)

8. His clothing would be divided by lots
   (Psalm 22:18 > Matthew 27:35)[159]

The fulfillment of this significant number of prophecies with such precise accuracy serves to establish, beyond any reasonable doubt, not only that Jesus was the Son of God, but that the Bible is also what it claims to be—the Word of God.

Dr. Peter Stoner, Professor Emeritus of Science at Westmont College in California, decided to assign his graduate students the task of calculating what the odds would be for these events to have happened by chance. Using just the eight prophecies listed above, not to mention the other 340+ (like His Davidic lineage, virgin birth, and no broken bones), he calculated that the odds would be 1 in 1017. A committee of the American Scientific Affiliation has verified these calculations.[160]

CURRENT FULFILLMENT OF PROPHECIES

Since more and more ancient biblical predictions are coming to pass in our time, not only is there admittedly supernatural phenomena taking place, but the evidence of divine inspiration is also growing stronger with time. The most notable prophecy coming to pass is the recent re-establishment of Israel as a nation in its ancient homeland.

It is impossible to accomplish what Israel has accomplished unless God sovereignly orchestrated such events. A nation that was destroyed as an organized entity by the invading Roman army in 70 AD, its people were either slaughtered or scattered throughout the world. Its land was then occupied and ruled by foreigners for 1900 years. Despite opposition and the scattering of their people in what is known as the Diaspora, the Jews somehow survived as a distinct nationality, never assimilating into the people groups where they lived. Although one never hears of a Canadian Moabite or an Italian Philistine, we have all heard of an American Jew or a Russian Jew. Then they finally regained their homeland again in 1948 and were recognized by most of the nations of the world. Perhaps what is most remarkable, though, is that Scripture predicted this amazing development over 2500 years before (Ezekiel 37:7-14; 38:8-12).[161]

SUMMARY

The evidence points not only to God's existence, but also to His authorship and inspiration of the Bible as well. No wonder it is so reliable. Following a logical train of thought, we can then begin to use Scripture as an authoritative guide to argue that what it says is true—particularly about the deity of Christ, creation, and the worldwide Flood. It is also fascinating to note that the Bible is unique from all other sacred writings because it is the only book that gives a continuous historical record from the first human being to the beginning of the Church Age. However, for the unconvinced skeptic, we will still continue to use rational means of argument for those topics in upcoming chapters.

Regarding the earlier illustration in this chapter, was the puzzle easily deciphered? It was probably challenging because all the vowels were missing. But now try reading it by inserting those missing vowels.

When one arbitrarily takes out all the vowels in a paragraph, then its message becomes very difficult to decipher. But when vowels are allowed to be included, then everything falls into place and the message makes perfect sense.

In the same way, when skeptics arbitrarily take God and the Bible out of consideration as they evaluate all that exists and what is true, then it is very difficult to decipher the answers to life's most formidable questions. But when God and the Scriptures are allowed to be a factor, everything else makes so much more sense.

It also brings clarity to the honest search for absolute truth. Without a reliable compass, one trekking through the journey of life can quickly lose their way. However, because the Bible is God's revelation to humankind regarding all aspects of life, one must only consult the Bible to find all the answers for which they are searching.

APPLICATION

We have asked a vital question in this chapter. Since it is reasonable to believe in one transcendent God, and since it is plausible that God would want to reveal Himself to humankind, how would that document look? The answer? A careful analysis of the content of the Bible demonstrates that it is a love letter from God to the prize of His creation—people. He has taken the initiative to reach out to us, who would otherwise be unable to know Him, and He has kindly introduced us to Himself. The ultimate theme in the Bible is about being reconciled to God and cultivating an intimate relationship with Him. All the historical people and events described in the Bible are just the structure that frames that sacred message.

The Bible is a very reliable historical document. And it is also divinely inspired.

CHAPTER 5

THE DEITY OF JESUS

KEY SCRIPTURES

Matthew 16:15-18 Then [Jesus] asked them, "But who do you say I am?" Simon Peter answered, "You are the Messiah, the Son of the living God." Jesus replied, "You are blessed, Simon son of John, because My Father in heaven has revealed this to you. You did not learn this from any human being."

Mark 14:61-64 Jesus was silent and made no reply. Then the high priest asked Him, "Are You the Messiah, the Son of the Blessed One?" Jesus said, "I am. And you will see the Son of Man seated in the place of power at God's right hand and coming on the clouds of heaven." Then the high priest tore his clothing to show his horror and said, "Why do we need other witnesses? You have all heard His blasphemy. What is your verdict?" "Guilty!" they all cried. "He deserves to die!"

John 10:38 If I do His work, believe in the evidence of the miraculous works I have done.

Mark 15:39 When the Roman officer who stood facing Him saw how He died, he exclaimed, "This Man truly was the Son of God!"

LEGEND, LIAR, LUNATIC, OR LORD

Over the past several chapters, we have seen that it is entirely reasonable to believe that one transcendent God does exist. It is also very conceivable that God reached out to engage humanity in relationship by inspiring various authors to write the Bible. In the remaining chapters, we will evaluate the plausibility of what the Bible says about Jesus, creation, and the presence of suffering and evil. In this chapter, we will discuss the central figure of the Bible's theme—Jesus Christ.

As soon as the name *Jesus* is mentioned, we enter into another realm of controversy. Though many people have strong opinions about Him, only facts should inform opinion, not personal preferences or biases. We must apply this evidence-based critical thinking when answering the question, "What is the most logical conclusion about who Jesus was?" Otherwise, avoiding this rational approach in favor of biased opinion immediately impugns one's credibility.

In Matthew 16:15-18 and in Mark 14:61-64, Jesus made the bold claim on two separate occasions that He is God. By doing so, Jesus did not leave us with an option to settle on the idea that He was just a good man with profound teachings. Even His enemies acknowledged that He claimed divinity. So, the question remains, "Was what Jesus said about Himself true, or was it not true?" Because Jesus declared that He is God, we have to decide whether or not we believe that He is who He said He is—God.

In answer to Jesus' question, "Who do you say that I am," there are only four alternatives. We must weigh all the evidence thoroughly to reach the most reasonable conclusion.[162]

First of all, either Jesus existed or not. If He did not exist, then He was quite a legend. But if He did live, then at least He is a historical figure.[163]

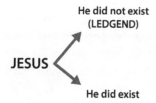

He did not exist
(LEDGEND)

JESUS

He did exist

1. LEGEND

There is no denying that Jesus was a historical figure. The witness accounts alone are staggering, from both His followers as well as His enemies. At least forty-three different authors, contemporary to Jesus' time, made references to Him—not only devout followers like Peter, James, and John, but also non-Christians, including Josephus, Tacitus, Tertullian, and even the Jewish Talmud.[164] Much of ancient history is based on fewer sources recorded much later than the events that they document. Jesus Christ, however, is one of the most-mentioned and most-substantiated lives in ancient times.[165]

Even so, some claim that, in the third and fourth centuries, enthusiastic followers of Jesus misinterpreted His statements, and that while He was a historical figure, He would be shocked to hear any connection to deity. In other words, while Jesus was indeed a real person who did exist, the claims of His divinity are merely legendary.

Arguments against the Legend theory

As we saw in chapter four, the overwhelming historical evidence implies that the New Testament, including what it says about the words and deeds of Jesus, is authentic and reliable. Modern archeology supports the fact that all four Gospel authors wrote their accounts within forty years of His death.[166] So, a mere legend gaining such wide circulation and impact is unfeasible. Imagine a biography of John Lennon written today, claiming that he thought he was God, forgave sins, and rose from the dead. Such a story would never gain any traction because there are too many people still living who knew enough about him to refute that claim.

For that reason, we can be convinced that the New Testament gives an accurate record of Jesus' claims. It is also important to remember that Jesus was not on trial for what He *did*, because He had done nothing wrong. Rather, He was on trial for what He *said* (John 10:30-33). The Gospels clearly communicate this fact, supported heavily by the uproar of the religious leaders and crowd at His trial. Suffice to say, Jesus was not a legend.

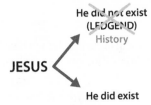

Thus, the claims of Jesus about Himself were either true or false. Again, only two alternatives remain.

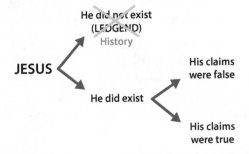

Let us suppose first that Jesus' claims about Himself were false. If they were false, then there are only two alternatives; either Jesus knew that His claims about Himself were false, or He did not know that His claims about Himself were false.

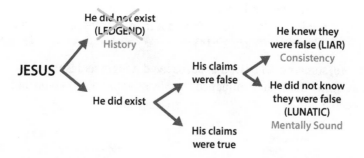

2. LIAR

If Jesus knew that His claims of divinity were false, then He was a *liar.* But if Jesus knew that He was not God, then He deliberately deceived His followers. This fraud would also make Him a *hypocrite,* then, because He told others to be honest, whatever the cost, while He taught and lived a colossal lie. And He would be *sinister* because He told others to trust in Him for their eternal destiny, knowing full well that He could never deliver. Furthermore, He would be a *fool* because His claims of holiness led to His crucifixion.[167] All He would have had to do was recant when the excruciating pain on the cross became too unbearable.[168] But He did not.

Arguments against the Liar theory

Eminent historian Philip Schaff stated, "How in the name of logic, common sense, and experience, could an imposter—that is a deceitful, selfish, depraved man—have invented, and consistently maintained from the beginning to end, the purest and noblest character in history with the most perfect air of truth and reality?"[169] Schaff goes on to observe that it would be impossible for such a man to conceive and successfully carry out a plan of unparalleled kindness and worldwide moral ramifications in every generation to follow. Furthermore, it would be impossible for such a man to penetrate the society of the Jews—a people with the strongest prejudices in all of history.[170] It is impossible to believe that such a man could endure the slow, agonizing death that Jesus suffered without breaking and denying His claims, unless He believed that

His claims were true and that His mission was purposeful. Lastly, even His enemies declared that He was a man of integrity and One who taught the truth (Mark 12:14).

Therefore, someone who lived as Jesus lived, taught as Jesus taught, died as Jesus died, and influenced as Jesus influenced, could not have been a liar.[171]

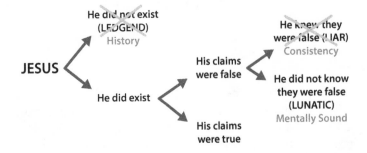

3. LUNATIC

If Jesus did not know that His claims were false, then He was a *lunatic*.[172] However, it is possible to be sincere, but sincerely wrong. Modern-day cult leaders like Jim Jones of the People's Temple and David Koresh of the Branch Davidians have willingly died believing the delusion that they were God.

But one would have to be severely deranged and insane to think of himself as God after being raised in a fiercely monotheistic culture such as Israel at the time of Jesus.

Arguments against the Lunatic theory

The skill and depth of His teaching support the fact that Jesus possessed total mental soundness.[173] Today, on the other hand, someone who claims divinity would likely be deemed insane. Yet, in Jesus, we do not observe the slightest hint of the abnormalities and imbalances associated with being mentally unstable. Jesus was never erratic in His behavior. He was distinguished by calmness and self-possession. He was also never vehement or expressed Himself passionately about His religious views.[174] He remained composed under pressure, serene, and never impatiently hurried into rash decisions.

Based on this evidence, we see that someone who spoke the most profound sayings ever recorded and who issued instructions that have even liberated many individuals from mental bondage could not have been a lunatic.[175]

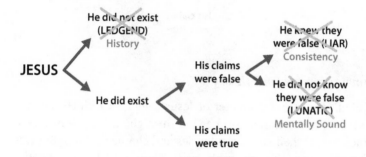

4. LORD

Since it is preposterous to conclude that the claims Jesus made about Himself were false due to the rational arguments presented above, then by logical reasoning, the claims that Jesus made about Himself must have been true. The only other sound alternative is that He is who He claimed to be—God (Lord).[176]

But anyone can make a claim. Many have claimed to be God throughout history. However, someone making such an outlandish declaration must be ready to support it with evidence. So, what would Jesus have had to do to prove that He is God? If He was just like any other individual, then He could not have been God. But in John 10:38, Jesus provided us the answer: "If I do His [the Father's] work, believe in the evidence of the miraculous works I have done, even if you don't believe Me. Then you will know and understand that the Father is in Me, and I am in the Father."

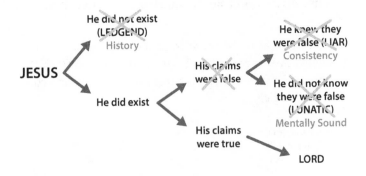

Arguments for the Lord theory

First of all, the moral character of Jesus coincides with His claims. Everyone who has claimed to be God throughout history has been contradicted by their sinful tendencies and character flaws. But this observation is not the case with Jesus. Those who lived with Him day in and day out for over three years testified to His sinless life, and they remained His devoted followers long after He ascended back to heaven.[177] Imagine a group of people living with anyone else that long. Surely someone, at some point, would find some short-comings that they possess. Still, not even those that opposed Jesus could find any fault in Him; not even Pilate after careful examination (Luke 23:4) or the experienced Roman centurion at the crucifixion (Mark 15:39).

Jesus also demonstrated power over natural forces and disease. The Gospels list 35 miracles that argue this point. Jesus, who exists as God and operated outside of the natural realm, intervened in the affairs of people frequently.[178] His ability to perform the supernatural is sound proof that He is God.

We find another credential of Jesus in His fulfillment of over 350 Old Testament prophecies uttered several hundred years before His birth.[179] Look how God deliberately narrowed down the odds: God told Noah that Jesus would be born through Shem, one of three sons, effectively eliminating 2/3 of the world population. Later, God told Abraham that Jesus would come through Isaac, his second of eight sons (Genesis 25:2). God told Isaac that Jesus would come through Jacob, his second of two sons. Then God told Jacob that Jesus would come through Judah, one of twelve sons—a slim 8% chance. Finally, God told Jesse that Jesus would come through David, his last of eight sons—another 12% chance. So, the probability of Jesus' precise lineage matching every Old Testament prophecy was an impossibly slim chance.

Furthermore, in 1012 BC, it was predicted by one Old Testament author that Jesus would be crucified—800 years before the Romans ever even introduced this kind of brutal execution.[180] Isaiah added that Jesus would be born of a virgin, something biologically impossible, unless supernatural. He also predicted that Jesus' people would reject Him, but that the Gentiles would accept Him. There would also be a forerunner—a voice crying in the wilderness. John the Baptist fulfilled that prophecy. And by Micah's divine foreknowledge, God selected Bethlehem—a population of less than a thousand residents—as the Messiah's birthplace. Daniel also prophesied the exact number of years before Jesus' birth, but then Haggai and Zechariah confirmed that it would take place before the Temple's destruction in AD 70. It is absolutely remarkable that Jesus was born in this extremely narrow time slot.[181] So, if Jesus was not the anticipated Messiah during that window of just a few short years, then who else could it have been? We don't have a record of anyone else.

Several more ramifications narrow the drama down even further. The Messiah would be betrayed by a friend for thirty pieces of silver, which would be cast on the Temple floor and be used to buy a potter's field. Incredibly, different authors uttered each portion of this prophecy at different times and places. And it all came true just as they predicted.

All of these predictions are still just a fraction of the many, many precise details that made up the exact address to identify God's Son, the Messiah, the Savior of the World. If Jesus was not the long-awaited Messiah, then there was no Messiah.

Some accuse the Old Testament of being written after the life of Jesus, arguing that the authors wrote its prophecies after the fact to match the historical narrative. However, archeological discoveries reject this notion. One of the most significant archeological finds, but certainly not the only one, was the Dead Sea Scrolls. Following Jesus' crucifixion, a Jewish monastic sect called the Essenes, fearing annihilation by the Romans, hid thousands of manuscript fragments of the Old Testament in sealed clay jars in caves approximately seven-and-a-half miles north of Jericho. These scrolls, dated hundreds of years before Christ, were discovered accidentally in 1947 when a young, Arab shepherd boy looking for a stray goat tossed a rock into a cave and heard the sound of shattered pottery.[182] And the rest is history. So, it is an absolute fact that Jesus fulfilled many prophecies that were made long before He ever lived on the earth, thus performing what no other human could ever do.

However, the crowning proof of Jesus' deity was in His resurrection from the dead. This miracle, the most crucial foundational stone of Christian doctrine, has yet to be refuted by the most intelligent and determined skeptics.[183] The next portion of this chapter will be devoted exclusively to that point.

SUMMARY

Jesus cannot be classified merely as a significant historical figure. We must decide whether He was a legend, liar, lunatic, or Lord. Because of His claims, there are no other options. Each soul must make their own choice—to either accept Jesus' claims or to reject Jesus' claims.

As demonstrated above, the evidence is clearly in favor of Jesus being Lord. Those who have taken the position that Jesus was not Lord—either that He was a legend, a liar, or a lunatic—must support their position with evidence. In attempting to address that challenge, one must forego personal preference. But no evidence as of yet has been presented to back up their position convincingly.

However, to know proof of Jesus from history is to only know Him from afar. It is only to know *about* Him. Yet, His life and teachings reveal that He intensely desired that every one of us would know Him personally. In fact, on the eve of His death, He prayed, "Father, the hour has come. Glorify Your Son... And this is the way to have eternal life—to know You, the only true God, and Jesus Christ, the one You sent to earth" (John 17:1-3).

One of the most powerful pieces of evidence that Jesus lived, died, and rose from the dead—that He is God—is the changed lives of His followers. This life-change was not limited to only His first disciples, but it extended throughout history. Millions of people have testified that they have come to know Him and that He miraculously transformed their lives.[184]

How else would God come to earth and reveal Himself to us? We can exhaust so much energy attempting to deny Jesus and disprove His existence, but we are presented with a powerful alternative. We have an invitation to open our hearts to Him, become intimately acquainted with Him, and discover His life-changing power.

THE RESURRECTION OF JESUS

Matthew 28:2-6 Suddenly there was a great earthquake! For an angel of the Lord came down from heaven, rolled aside the stone, and sat on it. His face shone like lightning, and his clothing was as white as snow. The guards shook with fear when they saw Him, and they fell into a dead faint. Then the angel spoke to the women. "Don't be afraid!" he said. "I know you are looking for Jesus, who was crucified. He isn't here! He is risen from the dead, just as He said it would happen."

John 11:25-26 Jesus told her, "I am the resurrection and the life. Anyone who believes in Me will live... [and] will never ever die."

Romans 1:4 [Jesus] was shown to be the Son of God when He was raised from the dead by the power of the Holy Spirit. He is Jesus Christ our Lord.

1 Peter 1:3 It is by [God's] great mercy that we have been born again, because God raised Jesus Christ from the dead.

In this portion of the chapter, we will investigate the crowning proof of Christianity—the bodily resurrection of Jesus Christ. Everything else that was said and done in the Bible, no matter how great or marvelous, is utterly secondary to the resurrection of Jesus in importance. If His resurrection did *not* take place, then Christianity is a false religion. But if His resurrection did take place, then Jesus is God and the Christian faith is absolutely true.[185] The apostle Paul, a 1st-century convert and follower of Jesus, summed it up well in his letter to the church in Corinth:

> **1 Corinthians 15:14** If Christ has not been raised, then all our preaching is useless, and your faith is useless.

Paul rested his entire case on the bodily resurrection of Jesus.[186] Therefore, let us examine the *Person* of the Resurrection, the *Proof* of the Resurrection, and the *Power* of the Resurrection.

1. THE PERSON OF THE RESURRECTION

In the last portion of this chapter, we saw that Jesus Christ, the Person of the Resurrection, is a very unique individual. But, interestingly, skeptics place Him in an impossible position. On the one hand, they say to prove that He was God, He would have had to do something that no other human could do—something miraculous. So, He did the impossible by rising from the dead, among many other signs and wonders. But on the other hand, opponents of Jesus' divinity argue that anything supernatural does not fit into this natural world; it would be impossible.

The Person of Jesus was truly extraordinary. Without money and weapons, Jesus lovingly conquered more people than Alexander, Caesar, Muhammad, and Napoleon combined. And without science or formal education, He shed more light on matters both human and divine than all the world's philosophers and scholars combined. Without eloquence, He also spoke such words of life as were never spoken before and produced greater effects than the world's best poets and orators. And without ever publishing a single line, He set more pens in motion and furnished more themes for speeches, works of art, and lines of music than a whole host of great men and women of ancient and modern times.[187]

Furthermore, Jesus never owned a home. He never held a public office. He never made a family of His own. He never went to college.

He never visited a big city. He did not surround Himself with the elite, but rather just a bunch of fishermen and other misfits. He never traveled more than two hundred miles from the place where He was born. And He could not boast of any credentials. Betrayed by His closest friends and with the tide of popular opinion turned against Him, Jesus was executed among criminals and buried in a borrowed tomb.

Still, twenty long centuries have come and gone, and today He is the centerpiece of the entire human race and the dominating Leader of the column of progress. Put together, all the armies that ever marched, all the navies that ever sailed, all the parliaments that ever sat, and all the kings that ever reigned have not affected humankind as powerfully as Jesus.[188]

2. THE PROOF OF THE RESURRECTION

If Jesus did not rise from the dead, then He is no different from all other great men who have also died. He would be no different from Confucius, Buddha, or Muhammad. On the other hand, if His resurrection is a demonstrable fact of history, then not only are His *claims* vindicated, but so are His *promises* also.[189] How does one determine if His resurrection is a fact or a legend? One must evaluate it as we do any event in history. Consider the following illustration:

On a cold, rainy Friday night, March 2, 1962, in Hershey Park, Pennsylvania, the Philadelphia Warriors were hosting the New York Knickerbockers in Hershey Arena as one of their home-away-from-home games to attract more fans. That night, Hall-of-Famer Wilt Chamberlain accomplished something that no other NBA player has ever come close to doing before that night or since. He set the NBA single-game scoring record by tallying 100 points! This feat is incredible considering that in most NBA games, neither *team* breaks a hundred points. Even though the Knicks started playing dirty as he neared the century marker, the #13 star center was still unstoppable. With 46 seconds left in the game, he sank a slam dunk from underneath for his 100th point, and play was halted for nine whole minutes as hundreds of fans raced onto the court. It is considered one of the greatest events in sports history.[190]

But did you personally watch that game? If not, how do you know what you just read is true? There were only 4,124 fans in attendance and there is no film footage. In fact, how do we know the truth about *any* event in history? What do we use as proof? There are specific rules of historicity that are so foundational that we do not even think about them. It is simple logic. First of all, all the fans served as eyewitnesses. And journalists also documented this incredible event right after it happened. So, because of these eyewitnesses and reporters, Chamberlain's 100-point game is considered a fact, even though most of us cannot prove it.

Similarly, we must examine the evidence for the resurrection of Jesus—another historical event—with the *same* criteria. We cannot allow the rules of historicity to be changed simply because the resurrection has religious overtones and implications. In studying history, one cannot construct a narrative from preconceived notions and adjust the evidence to fit a personal bias. Instead, one must reproduce the story from the best evidence and then let history speak for itself.

Remember, the word *apologetics* was initially a legal term—a defense in a court of law. So, how would one prove in court that an event ever occurred? Since events cannot be repeated and observed according to the scientific method, then a judge has to rely on forensic science. There are three testimonies common in any court of law according to forensics: 1) written testimony, 2) oral testimony, and 3) physical testimony. Was there anything written and recorded at the time of the event? Were there any observers of the event who were willing to make a statement? And were there any fingerprints or other physical aspects left at the scene of the event? This approach to discerning the truth about any historical event is commonly accepted worldwide in any court of law.[191]

Since the resurrection of Jesus is on trial in the minds of skeptics, then how does a Christian provide the evidence to substantiate the foundational claim of Christianity? He or she would have to evaluate it the same way one would measure any historical evidence: 1) written testimony, 2) oral testimony, and 3) physical testimony. The Christian apologist certainly has all of these testimonies readily at their disposal. This chapter proving the deity of Christ, including His miraculous resurrection, provides ample examples of those various legal proofs.

But can anyone prove with 100% certainty that anything ever happened historically? Do we have absolute proof that Julius Caesar crossed the Rubicon? Admittedly, no one can present 100% proof of any event that occurred in the past. But we do not have to have absolute, 100% evidence to make a decision. We make decisions every day simply based on the weight of the evidence—the probability that something happened or will happen. If we had to have absolute proof of our arrival at a destination before we ever started on a journey, then we would never even get into our vehicle. Similarly, juries would never convict someone if the prosecution had to produce 100% proof of their charge. But the prosecution only has to prove something beyond a reasonable doubt. So, although apologists do not have absolute proof for the resurrection of Jesus, or for any other biblical claim for that matter, they only need to demonstrate that the probability of the resurrection being true is very, very high. While it is not absolute (nothing historical is), it is undoubtedly sufficient.[192]

That said, Professor Thomas Arnold, a 14-year headmaster of Rugby University, author of a highly acclaimed, three-volume history book, and chair of Modern History at Oxford University, stated, "I have been used for many years to study the histories of other times, and to examine and weigh the evidence of those who have written about them, and I know of no one fact in the history of mankind which is proved by better and fuller evidence of every sort, than the great sign which God has given us that Christ died and rose again from the dead."[193]

A more recent professor of Ancient History, Dr. Paul Maier, who served at Western Michigan University, stated, "If all evidence is weighed carefully and fairly, it is indeed justifiable, according to the canons of historical research, to conclude that the tomb in which Jesus was buried was actually empty on the morning of the first Easter. And no shred of evidence has yet been discovered in literary sources, epigraphy, or archaeology that would disprove this statement."[194] (His last point is so important. Where is *any* evidence offered by skeptics to disprove the resurrection?)

Rules of Historicity

Like Chamberlain's 100-point game, we have ample testimony of many witnesses to the resurrection of Jesus. And to be proven valid and trustworthy, a testimony must meet three criteria in court and history:

1. First-hand knowledge, not just hearsay
2. The character of the witnesses must be sound and above reproach
3. Agreement of the testimonies of the various witnesses[195]

First of all, several of the New Testament writers certainly fulfill that criterion. Peter, James, John, and Matthew were all eyewitnesses of the empty tomb and wrote accordingly. Secondly, not even the severest critics question the sincerity and ethics of those witnesses. Thirdly, not only is there full harmony of all the accounts of the Resurrection, but the individual accounts also project it as a central truth and convey the absence of collaboration and collusion among themselves.

Furthermore, when studying an event in history, it is crucial to investigate whether enough eyewitnesses to the event were still living when the facts about the event were published. Their presence validates the accuracy of the published reports. Had the Resurrection been a concocted tale, many other witnesses would have readily come forward to dispute their accounts' accuracy. Yet, history remains silent.

Even so, many have proposed conspiracy theories to rationalize the events of the Resurrection apart from supernatural phenomena. For instance, some accuse the disciples of stealing the body. Others allege that Jesus never actually died; He just swooned. And then others maintain that on that early first Easter morning, the distraught women must have gone to the wrong tomb.

However, wishful alternative theories are not evidence. As we can see, Christians have ample, first-century proof for the Resurrection. The same cannot be said for alternative theories. In fact, they can easily be debunked because they are full of absurdities and improbabilities. Consider the two-ton boulder placed over the entrance of the tomb, the sixteen highly trained Roman guards posted outside the tomb, the absence of the disciples's prosecution for breaking the governor's seal, the efficiency of execution by Roman crucifixion (a 100% fatality rate), the airtight entombing process, and the local authorities who were highly motivated to correct any false claims.[196] These efforts make it very difficult for critics to defend the fragile position that Christ did *not* rise from the dead. The evidence is more than convincing.

3. THE POWER OF THE RESURRECTION

Jesus did not merely rise from the dead to make a statement. His resurrection holds the power to change lives. Immediately following the crucifixion, His band of followers was so frightened that they hid in fear. His apparent death shattered their hopes of a kingdom, and they were disheartened and confused. Yet, in Acts, we read about those same followers who were so courageous. Many of them emerged as prominent leaders among the bold followers that formed the Early Church. Being convinced of Jesus' bodily resurrection and being filled with the Holy Spirit's power made the difference in those followers' lives.

Through the ages, transformed lives continue. Let us consider one unlikely place today—Iran. Headlines report Iran's preparations for the Twelfth Imam, uranium stockpiles, and their intent to annihilate Israel. And radio pundits report the economic sanctions against Iran by the West to prevent further development of their nuclear arsenals. However, omitted from the media is the reality that more Iranians have celebrated the resurrection of Jesus in recent years than any other time in human history. More Iranians have renounced Islam and have become followers of Jesus in the last 35 years than the past 14 centuries combined, all with significant personal risk.[197] Why? Because there is such tremendous power in the Resurrection!

SUMMARY

Why are the Person, the Proof, and the Power of the Resurrection such vital points to argue? Because it is proof that Jesus changes our lives. The empty tomb gives us hope. It gives us hope beyond our next crisis, beyond death, and beyond this life. In His letter to the church gathering in Philippi, the apostle Paul wrote of the hope that the Resurrection provides:

> **Philippians 3:10-12** I want to know Christ and experience the mighty power that raised Him from the dead. I want to suffer with Him, sharing in His death, so that one way or another I will experience the resurrection from the dead!

For Paul, and for all of us, the life that Jesus lived qualified Him for the death He died. But the death that He died qualifies us for the life that we can live. Jesus Christ was the first-fruit of the Resurrection. A day is coming when Jesus will invite all who believed in Him and became His followers to live eternally with Him. And when that day comes, death will no longer have its grip on those who have been born again. Only the Person of the resurrection could ever do that feat. It is also only by the Proof of the Resurrection that we have our confidence. And it is by the Power of the Resurrection that we can ever experience it.

THE OUTRAGEOUS CLAIMS OF JESUS

In this chapter, we have seen how the evidence points overwhelmingly toward the divine nature of Jesus. It is reasonable to conclude that He is God. What else would God have had to have done to introduce Himself to the human race? He would have had to have done something that only God could do and that a person could not do. But we have seen that God certainly satisfied this criterion.

We also cannot be content with the two contradictory positions often presented—that He would have to perform miracles to prove He is God, but that the supernatural cannot take place in this natural world. We have to be consistent and logical in our reasoning.

As God, Jesus made some outlandish claims. At least, at first glance, it appears that way. Were these claims truly absurd? Or were they the most rational and life-giving statements ever uttered? Let us consider what Jesus said and evaluate it with a reasonable approach.

John 14:6 Jesus told him, "I am the way, the truth, and the life."

Amazingly, in just one short sentence, Jesus boldly cut against the grain of pop culture today and blatantly contradicted the central tenets of the postmodern worldview. By declaring to be the only **way** to God, Jesus challenged *pluralism*. By stating that He was the only source of **truth**, Jesus challenged *relativism*. And by maintaining that He was the only supply of real, fulfilling **life**, Jesus challenged *hedonism*.

In this day and age, such statements could be considered an act of war in some countries. What Jesus said is now regarded as offensive language that elicits a visceral response in many people. By these declarations, Jesus attacked the most cherished beliefs in all the other world religions. Some accuse Him of being arrogant, narrow-minded, and intolerant. To make such exclusive claims, "I am right, everybody else is wrong," also smacks of intolerance, religious chauvinism, and a superior attitude that ends up fostering hatred and violence. And it is considered to be politically incorrect, a verbal slap in the face, and socially unacceptable. Just as it is today, so it was in Jesus' day. People were so offended that they killed Him.

So, let us evaluate each statement by Jesus against the tide of public opinion, and let us just see what makes the most sense.

1. I AM THE WAY

Jesus said that the only way to get to God is through Him. He went on to say in that same verse, "No one can come to the Father except through Me." If anyone tried another way to be reconciled to God, then they would come up woefully short.

Pluralism, on the other hand, states that as long as one believes in a Higher Power and tries to be a good person, then it does not matter what religion to which one ascribes. There are different paths up the mountain, but they all lead to the same summit.[198] People who embrace this worldview maintain that we should emphasize all the common aspects of world religions, not the differences. A popular bumper sticker says, "coexist," featuring some of the different symbols of the various world religions.

We have seen prominent examples of this faulty notion. For instance, former UK Prime Minister Tony Blair founded the Faith Foundation, an ambitious effort to bring all world religions together. Additionally, The Yale Center published a document stating that Christians and Muslims worship the same God.[199] Ecumenicalism surrounds us. Some claim that all world religions are fundamentally the same and only superficially different. But in reality, they are fundamentally different and only superficially similar.

Before we consider the accusation that Christianity is exclusive and intolerant, it is important to understand that every world religion claims to be the only way; each religion claims exclusivity. Most of those religions are very intolerant of other faiths. Consider Islam, for example. Many nations that are predominantly Muslim—Pakistan, Saudi Arabia, and Iran—make it very difficult to subscribe to any other world religion. On the other hand, there is no Christian nation on earth where one's life is in danger because they subscribe to another faith. Hinduism is another prime example. It claims the ultimate authority rests in the *Vedas* and the caste system, and it is uncompromising about the law of karma and reincarnation. This belief system also persecutes believers of other faiths. It is not uncommon for a family to disown a son or daughter if they choose to marry someone who subscribes to another religion. Buddhists are also passionately exclusive of the exclusivists. Atheists, too, are intolerant toward those who claim to have faith, and they will even resort to censorship and intimidation if necessary. Therefore, to claim that Christianity is arrogant is inconsistent; every world religion claims to have a corner on the truth.

In this chapter, we have observed that the resurrection of Jesus can be proven true and establishes Him as being the Son of God. Since this fact is true, then other faith systems cannot be true since each one asserts ideas contrary to His divinity. So, is it possible to be sincere, but sincerely wrong? Of course, one can. Does pluralism make logical sense? No. Consider the following illustration:

A university professor decides to invite his class to his house for a cookout. He will provide all the food; the students simply have to show up hungry. Of course, the students ask the professor the obvious question, "Where do you live?" But what if the professor responds, "Oh, directions are overrated. It would be too closed-minded. Just take any road you wish; you will eventually wind up there." Using these instructions, how many students will arrive at his home? They might keep driving aimlessly, becoming more and more lost. The reality is that the professor lives on a cul-de-sac; there is only one road to his house. If the students miss that road, then they miss the cookout. This fact is not being closed-minded, bigoted, or arrogant. It is merely the practical truth.

In the same way, there is only one road that leads to God—Jesus Christ. Since all other world religions are contradictory, then one will sadly get further and further lost in their search for God by pursuing any other faith road.

Remember the four fundamental questions of life—origin, meaning, morality, and destiny? Only one Person has ever been able to answer all four of those questions in such a way as to correspond so consistently with reality. There is total coherence among His answers that is unlike those of any other religion. So, the Bible teaches that the highway to heaven has been closed for centuries. God did not set up the roadblock; we did because of our sin and self-sufficiency. The barriers that we erected were immovable, at least by us. But Jesus was the only One who could remove the barriers and open the way, and He willingly did so on the Cross. It is a narrow road, but we just have to choose it.

2. I AM THE TRUTH

Jesus also pointed to Himself as the only truth. He said that His very purpose for coming into the world was to testify to the truth (John 18:37). But what is truth? Truth is "that which conforms to reality."[200] Etymologically, the word *truth* comes from the same Germanic root as the word *tree*.[201] The implied meaning refers to something firm, fixed, and immovable. If one collides their car into a tree, then their bumper will have to conform to it because it will not budge. Truth is *objective* (it exists outside of ourselves, regardless of what we think). Truth is *absolute* (it is the same in every place every time). Truth is *universal* (what works for one works for everyone).

Relativism, conversely insists that no fact can be considered universally true at all times, in all places, and for all people.[202] This faulty worldview is growing rapidly. In fact, surveys show that the majority of Americans now espouse this idea.[203] It is no wonder that the Bible claims that people *turn away from* the truth (2 Timothy 4:3-4), *suppress* the truth (Romans 1:18), *distort* the truth (Acts 20:30), *reject* the truth (Romans 2:8), and *exchange* the truth for a lie (Romans 1:15).

Two thousand years later, not much has changed in our postmodern world. The common sentiment today is that truth is unknowable. Most people claim that what is known is *subjective* (it is whatever we want to make it), *relative* (it changes with every circumstance and situation), and *individualized* (whatever works for one person does not have to work for someone else). As a result, people can select elements from various belief systems, like one would in a restaurant buffet, customizing their belief system to suit themselves. Interestingly, the one thing people are absolutely sure of is that there are no absolutes (which is obviously an irrational contradiction).

But does relativism make sense? Is it logical to adhere to the absence of a source of truth derived outside of ourselves? Another university professor conducted an experiment with her class. She told the students to stand up and close their eyes. She then instructed them to face and point in the direction they thought was north. Finally, the professor asked all of them to take three paces forward in the same direction. Of course, because the students were going in different directions, confusion mounted quickly as they all collided into each other. The point was that "north" exists as a fact outside of ourselves. We are incapable of finding north within us. We need a compass, an objective measurement of the truth. Otherwise, confusion reigns. Likewise, just as a compass points north, the Bible points to truth and provides us with peace, clarity, and order.

We can apply this idea of a standard having to exist objectively outside of ourselves to so many different scenarios. Imagine a builder attempting to build a house but preventing all of his contractors from using a measuring tape, leaving them to measure everything based on what they *think* an inch and a foot should be. Imagine the instability once the structure is partially built but impossible to complete. We can apply the same conclusion to society. When one person's moral standard varies from another's, then the entire society becomes unstable.

One can make the same application to a pilot flying without instruments or to a crowded city disregarding all the traffic laws. Clearly, standards of measurement upon which everyone agrees must exist outside of ourselves. A reality must exist that is objective, universal, and absolute. Otherwise, civilization, as we know it, fails and becomes unsustainable. It is not up for a vote; it is unchanging. Jesus claimed to be that only Source of a fixed standard of moral measurement.

3. I AM THE LIFE

Jesus said that only He could provide abundant life. He also said, "My purpose is to give them a rich and satisfying life" (John 10:10b). In both verses, John 14:6 and John 10:10, Jesus did not use the typical Greek word *bios* that we find in other parts of Scripture. Instead, He used the word *zoe*. While *bios* means the most common form of life, the life of the physical body. *Zoe* means something far broader. It describes the fullness of life, both essential and ethical, that manifests itself with vigor and activity, and implies a life blessed in every way.

Is that not the kind of life that drives all of us? How many times do the media and marketing firms use the word "extreme?" How often do we try to take our senses to hyper levels in entertainment so that we can, at least for a brief moment, experience the most out of life? Jesus, on the other hand, promises that if we abide by His ways, which are higher (and often opposite) than our ways, then we will, in fact, have an enriching, fulfilled, and overflowing life. Jesus says that if we manage our appetites and our passions, and exercise some self-discipline, then and only then will this kind of life be truly rewarding for us.

On the other hand, *hedonism* is the opposite of what Jesus offers and permeates every aspect of our culture today. Sadly, the world argues vehemently against what Jesus has to offer. Most people are on varying degrees of the spectrum. Pure hedonism claims that pleasure is the only intrinsic good. It focuses not only on the absence of pain, but also on the piquing of all our sensations. The supreme goal in life with this worldview is contentment.[204] A pain-free life seems to be such an inherent right today that people tend to blame God if things do not go exactly the way they wish. For example, someone might follow this kind of reasoning: "I have a right to have a grandmother; I am entitled. But my grandmother died. So, it is God's fault because He could have prevented her from dying. God violated me. Therefore, I will not serve God." In the naturalist worldview, there is also nothing wrong with sensual, excessive indulgences. As the familiar adage goes, "If it feels good, then do it." We ought to be able to give full vent to our lusts and passions and do all that we can to satisfy those insatiable appetites. TV advertising subtly conditions us with incessant messaging, "If you want it, then you can have it."

But unbridled hedonism is dangerously destructive both to individuals as well as to society at large. This basal "live for yourself and not for others" mentality is the epitome of selfishness, making any person no longer attractive. Victims are always not too far behind those who live only for themselves, gratifying their base impulses. Hedonism is actually paradoxical because it is detrimental to long-term happiness. True contentment is ever elusive. Interestingly, pleasure-seekers somehow always end up in despair.[205] It is like saltwater—the more one indulges, the more one craves. The more one attempts to satisfy, the more one has to satisfy. It is addictive. We see this sad reality exemplified in those who use stimulants and have become co-dependent. Excessive consumers always end up being less happy than temperate consumers. Overindulgence always leads to moral decay, which then ultimately leads to painful consequences.

More than one nanny for the rich and famous has published tell-all articles and interviews about what life is really like behind closed doors regarding family dynamics in an excessive lifestyle. Marriages are usually tense, and children are often spoiled, which makes for a very miserable life. And several well-known celebrities have ended their lives tragically early, not because of mental illness, but because they realized that all the fame and fortune that this world has to offer simply does not work without other key ingredients to life. But Jesus offers something far better even though it is counter-intuitive to our base nature as humans.

SUMMARY

Even though it is unpopular in secular circles today, when we consider all of the alternatives, we see that Jesus is just who He said He is—the way, the truth, and the life. In fact, He is the only way, the only truth, and the only life. So, out of care and concern for others, Christians must see themselves as apologists and lovingly lead those in their realm of influence to this liberating truth. In doing so, they will serve them best.

Can we know with absolute certainty that Jesus is alive today and wants to redeem people? Yes, we can know for sure! There is a difference between proving something absolutely and knowing something absolutely. Once someone stands upon the solid foundation of evidence and takes a step of faith to accept Jesus, then the Holy Spirit confirms in one's heart that which they now believe is true.

> **2 Corinthians 1:22** He has identified us as His own by placing the Holy Spirit in our hearts as the first installment that guarantees everything He has promised us.

So, we can know with certainty that Jesus is true beyond the certainty with which we have to prove it.[206]

CHAPTER 6

THE TRUSTWORTHINESS OF CREATION

KEY SCRIPTURES

Genesis 1:1 In the beginning, God created the heavens and the earth.

Exodus 20:11 For in six days the Lord made the heavens, the earth, the sea, and everything in them...

John 1:1-3 In the beginning, the Word [Jesus] already existed... God created everything through Him, and nothing was created except through Him.

Colossians 1:16-17 Through [Jesus], God created everything in the heavenly realms and on earth. He made the things we can see and the things we cannot see... Everything was created through Him and for Him. He existed before anything else, and He holds all creation together.

Hebrews 11:3 By faith we understand that the entire universe was formed at God's command, that what we now see did not come from anything that can be seen.

CONTEXT AND IMPORTANCE OF THE CREATION WORLDVIEW

The study of origins is critical because it attempts to answer two of the four basic questions of life that provide meaning to everything else in our world—*where did we come from,* and *why are we here?* If we are just mere products of random, impersonal processes, then we have no intrinsic value and purpose for our existence. On the other hand, if we were placed here by God for a specific purpose (an intimate relationship with Him and to be the object of His infinite affection), then we most certainly have infinite value and meaning. In this chapter, to equip the Christian with a sound defense of a proper understanding of our origins, we will compare the two major worldviews—creation and evolution. Comparing the two side-by-side and examining all of the evidence, we will determine which view makes more rational sense.

1. BOTH VIEWS BEGIN AT THE EXACT SAME PLACE— EVERYTHING CAME FROM NOTHING.

Admittedly, those who believe in creation require faith because it does not fit into the limited framework of empirical science. The moment of humanity's initial origin cannot be observed or repeated. Furthermore, the law of cause and effect states that for every effect, there must have been an adequate cause; everything must have come from something. Creationists have no absolute proof for the Cause of all the effects that we can observe today. "By faith we understand that the entire universe was formed at God's command (Hebrews 11:3). Thus, creationism is reduced to a theory.

But by the same token, those who believe in evolution also require faith since their views cannot be proven by classical empirical science. Not only does evolution violate the Law of Cause and Effect, but its premise of macro-evolution also cannot be observed or repeated. Evolutionists have no absolute proof either for the initial cause of all the effects observed today. Therefore, evolution is reduced to a theory that requires faith as well—a lot of faith.

Any belief that requires faith is deemed more religious than scientific. The fact that evolution requires faith is one reason that Atheism is recognized worldwide as an official religion. The US Supreme Court deemed Atheism a religion that is protected under the First Amendment of the US Constitution in their landmark *Torcaso v. Watkins* (1961) decision.[207]

So, a creationist should not feel inferior to an evolutionist simply because they possess faith in concepts they cannot prove. Evolutionists face the same challenge. Both worldviews start at the same place—faith.

2. BOTH VIEWS HAVE SOURCES FOR THEIR AUTHORITY.

The source of authority for creationists is the Bible. The source of authority for evolutionists is Charles Darwin's *On the Origin of Species by Means of Natural Selection (Origin of Species)*. Let us compare what these sources of authority say:

Genesis 1:1 In the beginning, God created...

John 1:1-3 In the beginning was the Word (Jesus)... God created everything through Him, and nothing was created except through Him.

Colossians 1:16-17 For through Him (Jesus) God created everything in the heavenly realms and on earth. He made the things we can see and the things we can't see... Everything was created through Him and for Him. He existed before anything else, and He holds all creation together.

Hebrews 11:3 By faith we understand that the entire universe was formed at God's command, that what we now see did not come from anything that can be seen.

So, Scripture is very clear regarding our origins. It claims that a divine act by God brought the world into ordered existence (creation).

The opposing view of evolution states that a gradual process of change has occurred as life sprang from non-life, with living organisms increasing in complexity over time.[208] Charles Darwin believed that all animals and plants descended from one prototype.[209] In other words, evolutionists claim that *unknown* chemicals in an *unknown* past, which cannot be verified, through *unknown* processes which no longer exist, produced *unknown* life forms that are not to be found, but somehow could, through *unknown* reproductive methods, spawn new life in an *unknown* atmospheric composition, in an *unknown* ocean-like soup complex, at an *unknown* time and at an *unknown* place.[210] With all of those unknown variables, no wonder this notion requires such a leap of faith.

However, since Darwin published his book over 150 years ago, many of the faith claims in his book have been disproven as advances in science have been made. Therefore, it is ceasing to be the authority for many, even though they still are not prepared to concede that God exists. Conversely, as we concluded in an earlier chapter, archeological excavations and discoveries continue to validate the Bible.

Now, let us continue to examine both views.

3. BOTH VIEWS OFFER A CAUSE FOR ALL OF THE EFFECTS IN THE WORLD.

> **Genesis 1:2-3** The earth was formless and empty... Then God said, "Let there be light," and there was light.

And God continued to declare "Let there be..." fourteen times in Genesis 1, putting His omnipotent creative powers to work. For creationists, God is the Cause for all the effects in the universe.

On the other hand, in his sixth revised edition of the *Origin of Species*, Darwin suggested that "new and simple forms are continually being produced by spontaneous generation."[211] This statement was unsupported since he even prefaced it by stating that "science ha[d] not as yet proved the truth of this belief."[212] So, for evolutionists, spontaneous generation is the cause of all the effects in the universe.

Thus, two theories compete against each other—divine creation versus spontaneous generation. Notice that the premise for both views is *ex nihilo*—"everything out of nothing." Creation states that *Someone* was responsible for creating everything out of nothing; evolution says that *no one* was responsible for creating everything out of nothing. One view requires a *supernatural* intervention; the other view requires an *unnatural* intervention.[213] Both views are outside of the realm of empirical science that requires observability and repeatability. Therefore, both views fall within forensic science, which seeks to understand the "how" behind a one-time event. Again, since both creation and evolution require faith, then which theory is more plausible upon thorough examination, given the laws of science that we have at our disposal? And which approach requires the greatest leap of faith?

Darwin's statement reveals his determination to prove his theory despite the sound, scientific evidence otherwise. He wrote the above statement in 1872, thirteen years after his first edition in 1859. Interestingly, during the same year of his first edition, 1859, French microbiologist and chemist Louis Pasteur also disproved spontaneous generation. The French Academy of Science sponsored a science fair where Pasteur submitted his award-winning experiment, proving that microorganisms are airborne. By comparing two flasks of broth—one covered and the other uncovered—the uncovered flask gradually contained microbial life. Pasteur proved that life is transferred from elsewhere through the air, not spontaneously generated out of nothing.[214] Even though Darwin knew that scientific evidence refuted his theory over a decade before, he published his ideas regardless, failing to adapt his conclusions in future editions as discoveries were made. Today, the theory of evolution contradicts a fundamental principle of science. The law of biogenesis insists that new life can only come from existing life. Non-life cannot produce life.[215]

4. BOTH VIEWS DEAL WITH GENETIC INFORMATION.

Genesis 2:2: On the seventh day God had finished His work of creation, so He rested from all His work.

In the creationist's view, all of God's creative work ceased at the conclusion of creation week. In other words, all of the information necessary for creation was present on that seventh day; no new information was introduced afterward or ever since. Creation has not continued; the complete set of information has merely been rearranged from generation to generation. Furthermore, the initial Cause for all the effects that would occur in subsequent generations in the universe was completely adequate; all of the effects that we observe today cannot be greater in complexity than their original cause. Otherwise, some effects would be uncaused, which is logically irrational. The foundational law of science, the law of causality, provides all the support needed for this view.[216]

At this point, the trains of thought between the two worldviews diverge. Charles Darwin stated in *Origins of Species*, "I believe that all animals and plants are descended from one prototype."[217] In other words, evolutionists believe that new genetic information is continually being introduced into the gene pool, producing new and more advanced types of animals and plants from the original. They propose that the effects that we observe today did not necessarily have a cause and that there may be more future effects that do not have a cause in existence today. In light of known scientific laws and rationality, this belief requires a substantial leap of faith. However, this component is foundational in the theory of evolution.

Consider, for instance, the opposable thumb that is characteristic to monkeys and humans—a finger that can cross the palm to enhance one's grip of a tool. Creationists believe that God provided all the genetic information for a thumb in the first man and woman, Adam and Eve; it did not eventually come later. Therefore, all humans have a thumb, unless a genetic mistake happens and some information is lost, resulting in the rare occurrence of an individual born without a thumb.[218] However, as soon as that person mates with another person, then the thumb reappears in the next generation because the information from the union is recovered.

Evolutionists, on the other hand, believe that the information for a thumb has been introduced over time as a higher form of complexity.[219] But this view begs the question: from where did this genetic information initially come? This perplexing question is unanswerable; it is an uncaused effect, which contradicts the laws of science.

Even Darwin himself admitted to this leap of faith. If living organisms gradually evolved from simple life to complex life over time, then we would observe gradual changes in the fossil record. However, the fossil record reveals distinct organisms neatly separated into distinct kinds. To that point, Darwin stated, "If it could be demonstrated that any complex organ[ism] existed, which could not possibly have been formed by numerous, successive, slight modifications, my theory would absolutely break down."[220] Since he made this statement more than 125 years ago, science has demonstrated that numerous, successive, and slight modifications did not form *all* existing complex organisms. So, by his admission, Darwin's theory has indeed broken down.

5. BOTH VIEWS DEAL WITH THE MIGRATION OF GENETIC INFORMATION.

Genesis 1:21-25 God created great sea creatures and every living thing that scurries and swarms in the water, and every sort of bird—each producing offspring of the same kind... Then God said, "Let the earth produce every sort of animal, each producing offspring of the same kind—livestock, small animals that scurry along the ground, and wild animals." And that is what happened. God made all sorts of wild animals, livestock, and small animals, each able to produce offspring of the same kind.

Seven times in six verses, the Bible says, "of the same kind" or "according to its kind," depending upon the translation. The Bible clearly intends for us to know that there would never be any migration of genetic information between kinds.

This phenomenon of organisms reproducing according to their kind is undoubtedly present and observable. Dogs make dogs; cats make cats. We never see a dog accidentally looking like a partial cat. Nor is it conceivable for a fish gill to evolve into a reptile lung and then again into a bird lung over time. Each of these organisms is *irreducibly complex*. If any transitional variation occurs at all, then the lungs cease to function, and the organism dies before it is ever able to reproduce.[221] This fact is true for every organ in all living beings.

Organs such as lungs can be compared to a mousetrap. There are only a few pieces of this familiar tool—a base, a spring, a neck-breaker, and a piece that holds the neck-breaker in place. How many parts would have to be missing to render the mousetrap ineffective? Only one. All of the components in this contraption are interdependent.[222] The same is true for organs in animals; anything partial or transitional would not work and render the animal dead.

Additionally, there is no evidence found in the fossil record that suggests any links between kinds.[223] Furthermore, the oldest records in the world, drawings of animals found in Egyptian hieroglyphics, show no signs of change when compared to modern-day animals.[224]

Even so, despite the lack of evidence, Darwin published concepts like "slow and gradual modification through descent and natural selection" because he had adopted the notion of *transmutations*.[225] Although unobservable and unrepeatable, the concept of trans-mutations is essential for the atheistic model of evolution to work.

Transmutations are merely hypothetical, have never been observed, and violate the fundamental laws of science as well. No observational evidence has ever shown that genera evolve into families and families into orders, and so on.[226] For instance, it is impossible for the genes of a cat to be compatible with the genes of a dog. It is also impossible for the genes of a chimpanzee to be compatible with the genes of a human being. Not only are they unable to produce a hybrid offspring, but they also contain contrasting languages at the DNA level.[227] Furthermore, while a cow can grow a fifth leg in a very rare case (a mutation), it is impossible for a cow to grow a turtle shell. The genetic information that exists in a turtle does not exist in a cow. And there is no possible way for that information to transfer from the turtle to the cow. So there are firm genetic limits on how far an organism can change.[228] Darwin himself admitted that species are *immutable*; they are unchanging.[229] But he hoped that with the advancement of science, evidence of transmutations would eventually be discovered, substantiating his atheistic views.

Similarities between different kinds—for instance, between apes and humans—do not necessarily suggest a common ancestor as

Darwin maintained. Rather, they could just as easily suggest a common Artist.[230] Just as Rembrandt demonstrated unique characteristics and similarities among his paintings (as did Picasso, Van Gogh, and Monet), so the unique characteristics and similarities between kinds make a stronger case for a common Creator rather than a common cell. Yes, there are anatomical similarities between monkeys and people, but the differences between the two kinds are so vast that it would be impossible to share a common ancestor.

Thus, all available forensic evidence points to creationism as the most plausible explanation, leaving evolution as a much weaker alternative. Since transmutations are illogical, then the theory of evolution cannot continue to develop. Still, let us continue to follow the two opposing trains of thought.

6. ONE VIEW INSISTS WE ARE DEVOLVING; THE OTHER VIEW INSISTS THAT WE ARE EVOLVING.

> Genesis 3:2-3,17 "Of course we may eat fruit from the trees in the garden," the woman replied [to the serpent]. "It's only the fruit from the tree in the middle of the garden that we are not allowed to eat. God said, 'You must not eat it or even touch it; if you do, you will die.'" And to the man [God] said, "Since you listened to your wife and ate from the tree whose fruit I commanded you not to eat, the ground is cursed because of you."

According to this verse, man's willful disobedience to God resulted in a death sentence for all creation. Everything is running down— from vitality toward a lifeless equipoise. This view aligns perfectly with another well-known law of science—the second law of thermodynamics.[231] As energy and matter are being spent during natural processes, they are reduced to less usable forms. Because of entropy, everything is seeking the lowest level of equilibrium.[232]

However, the premise of evolution is quite the opposite. According to its proponents, the world is developing into more complex forms through heritable traits, mutations, adaptations, and natural selection.[233]

The evolution of the opposable thumb referenced and disproven earlier is often referred to in both "adaptation" and "survival of the fittest" ideology. Consider, however, binocular vision found in monkeys and humans (two eyes facing forward) as well as bipedalism in humans (walking uprightly). According to evolutionists, these traits were originally mutations, mistakes in the genetic code.[234] They argue that because these mutations make the new organism superior in the competition for survival, they eventually became prominent because of their advantage. Those who could not adapt eventually became extinct.

However, there are several problems with this assumption. First of all, mutations are seldom beneficial; they are genetic malfunctions that are almost always harmful, destructive, and often fatal. So, rather than forming more complex, higher forms of life, mutations indicate a loss of information, which would mean a less complex, lower life form. A change occurs in the organism, but it is always in the wrong direction. Never does new information arise in a mutation. The viability of the organism decreases; it never increases. In a rare instance, an organism can lose genetic information and gain some function. But for the evolutionary view to be supported, there would need to be millions of these instances. Obviously, this unlikely development has not ever happened.[235] In fact, the existence of mutations supports the Second Law of Thermodynamics and the Curse found in Genesis 3:17-19. Mutations do not support evolution since the organisms become less suited to cope with their environment's stress and less competitive for survival.

As stated earlier, mutations can only occur within kinds, but never across kinds. Furthermore, if everything did evolve from one prototype, then there should be no gaps among kinds. There should be no distinct, separate forms of living organisms.[236] If all organisms evolved from a common ancestor, then they should all be interconnected and possess the ability to interbreed easily.

Thus, the stability of the present, observable, repeatable genetic process for the entire animal and plant kingdoms reinforces creationism and soundly refutes evolutionism.

Darwin himself struggled with this concept. He queried, "Why, if species have descended from other species by fine gradations, do we not everywhere see innumerable transitional forms? Why is not all of nature in confusion, instead of the species being as we see them—well-defined?"[237]

Darwin went on to confess in the *Origin of Species*, "If my theory be true, numberless intermediate varieties, linking all the species together, must assuredly have existed. Why then is not every geological formation full of such intermediary links? Geology assuredly does not reveal any graduated chain; and this, perhaps, is the most obvious and gravest objection which can be urged against my theory."[238] It would behoove evolutionists today to consider all of Darwin's observations, not just ideas that have been refuted by the laws of science.

CONCLUSION

We can see that by comparing the first chapter of the Bible to the statements made throughout the *Origin of Species*, science does not contradict the Bible, but it does contradict evolution. In fact, we have observed throughout this book that evolution contradicts the law of causality, the law of biogenesis, the law of probability, the laws of thermodynamics, the law of heredity (genetics), as well as several other laws of science, the Fossil Record, and 90% of the dating methods. These principles are not just theories; they are well-established laws of science accepted by scientists across the entire spectrum of perspectives. On the other hand, those who espouse that the God of the Bible is the Intelligent Designer of the universe embrace those laws, and their views are consistent with them. Creationists have science on their side. So, it is safe to conclude that creation is the most logical worldview that requires the least assumptions.

Both views are incredible; they both suggest "everything from nothing." One is unnatural; the other is supernatural. Since neither can be repeated or observed, then neither view can fall under empirical science. However, since we have to look for clues after the fact to explain our origins, then both views fall well within the realm of forensic science.

The problem for atheists is that creation acknowledges God's role. And to admit to His existence is to surrender one's self-rule and to accept the rules that God has set in place for humanity's behavior instead. This issue is at the heart of the ongoing insistence that evolution should be the alternative to creation.

Finally, if people are simply products of random, impersonal processes, as evolutionists suggest, then people should have no more value than a tree or a bug. But on the other hand, if every person on the planet was created by a loving God to be the object of His affection, as creationists suggest, then a person's life is extremely valuable—it is priceless.

The Bible suggests *anthropocentrism* (from the Greek, meaning "human being center"), that humans are the most important entity in the universe. The more familiar term is commonly known as *human exceptionalism*. This belief is founded upon Genesis 1 and Psalm 8:

> **Genesis 1:26** Then God said, "Let Us make human beings in our image, to be like Us. They will reign over the fish in the sea, the birds in the sky, the livestock, all the wild animals on the earth, and the small animals that scurry along the ground."

> **Psalm 8:4-8** What are mere mortals that You should think about them, human beings that You should care for them? Yet You made them only a little lower than God and crowned them with glory and honor. You gave them charge of everything You made, putting all things under their authority—flocks and the herds and all the wild animals, the birds in the sky, the fish in the sea, and everything that swims the ocean currents.

According to Scripture and the view that best corresponds with reality, human beings are distinctly different from animals. Not only are people created in the image and likeness of God, but they also possess a consciousness that is absent in all other animals.[239] People were created with the capacity and purpose to have an intimate relationship with God; animals were not.

But the secular worldview suggests that the material world is all that there is and that there is nothing metaphysical about us to set us apart from other animals. God is not part of the equation. However, the problem with such a position is that it fails to uphold the intrinsic nature of human dignity, liberty, and equality. It also falls woefully short of recognizing fundamental human rights and responsibilities. But without these moorings, a wide range of bioethical issues are ignored. What then is to prohibit assisted suicide, euthanasia, embryonic stem cell research, human genetic manipulation, human cloning, human trafficking, slavery, racism, feminine oppression, radical environmentalism, subjugation of the poor, child labor, and the far-reaching animal rights movement?[240] Removing God from ethics is a slippery slope into a steep moral decline.

So, what does the evidence show? The fact that life is considered sacred by every culture on every continent of the globe has to be a serious consideration. Murder is universally wrong in every country, regardless of political ideology. Furthermore, everyone possesses an innate drive for self-preservation. Life is sacred. But from where did this value come? The notion of random, impersonal origins is inconsistent with the universal intrinsic value upon human life. And the fact that even atheists value life is contradictory. Thus, the infinite value upon human life is yet another reason to believe that life was created on purpose—created by God who places infinite value upon human life.

CHAPTER 7

THE VALUE OF PAIN AND SUFFERING

KEY SCRIPTURES

Romans 8:20-22 Against its will, all creation was subjected to God's curse. But with eager hope, the creation looks forward to the day when it will join God's children in glorious freedom from death and decay. For we know that all creation has been groaning as in the pains of childbirth right up to the present time.

Romans 8:28 We know that God causes everything to work together for the good of those who love God and are called according to His purpose for them.

Hebrews 12:7,9,11 As you endure divine discipline, remember that God is treating you as His own children. Who ever heard of a child who is never disciplined by its father? Since we respected our earthly fathers who disciplined us, shouldn't we submit even more to the discipline of the Father of our spirits, and live forever? No discipline is enjoyable while it is happening—it's painful! But afterward there will be a peaceful harvest of right living for those who are trained in this way.

INTRODUCTION

Thus far, we have seen that there is no logical escape from the causal argument for God. Once we thoroughly examine the evidence, it is reasonable to conclude that it requires more faith to be an atheist than to believe in one, transcendent, personal God, the Creator of the Universe. Failing in that argument, it seems that atheists and skeptics tend to take refuge in a popular *diversionary argument*, thinking that the discovery of a flaw in God's character will somehow suffice to prove His non-existence.[241]

In fact, the single biggest obstacle for spiritual seekers is this question: "If God is so loving, and if God is so powerful, then why does He allow so much evil and suffering to exist?"[242] Researcher George Barna conducted a national survey in which he asked a scientifically selected cross-section of adults, "If you could ask God only one question and you knew He would give you an answer, then what would you ask?" The top response was the question above. Here is how the rationale behind the perplexing question unfolds: If God is all-loving, then He should be willing to alleviate my pain. And if God is all-powerful, then He should also be capable of alleviating my pain. But since pain, suffering, and evil still exist in my life, then God must be neither willing nor capable nor both. Perhaps God does not exist. Or if He does, then He is malevolent and unworthy of any allegiance. Hence, God's existence is not what is actually on trial; it is His character.[243]

This problem is the age-old question that demands an answer. As far back as the fourth century BC, Epicurus, the ancient Greek philosopher, mused, "Either God wants to abolish evil but cannot; or He can abolish evil, but wants not. If He wants to, but cannot, then He is impotent. If He can, and wants not, then He is wicked. But, if God can and wants to abolish evil, then why is evil in the world?"[244]

It was precisely this obstacle that once tripped up a theology student in seminary, training to be a minister. When his beloved daughter, Annie, died of scarlet fever at the young age of ten, his faith in God was utterly shattered. He would later write that this period chimed the final death knell for his Christianity. This event drove Charles

Darwin to research our origins without God in the equation, ultimately writing *On the Origins of Species*.[245]

Similarly, another man lost his faith due to this same barrier. Like Darwin, he was a deeply religious man with plans to become a missionary. But when his younger sister, Mary Jane, contracted lupus and suffered terribly before dying, he turned the other way, becoming openly hostile to Christianity for the rest of his life. Today, Ted Turner is the billionaire media mogul who founded CNN—a network unapologetic about its hostility toward the Christian faith.[246]

A more recent example of this tragic stumbling block is what happened to the late Steve Jobs. This highly innovative entrepreneur revolutionized the digital world with the iPod, iPhone, iPad, and the online iTunes Store, marketed the first personalized computer, and turned Pixar into a billion-dollar conglomerate that produced countless box office hits like *Finding Nemo* and *Toy Story*. In the best-selling biography *Steve Jobs*, noted biographer Walter Isaacson recounts an event when the 13-year-old Jobs was distressed by a photograph in a 1968 issue of *Life* magazine. The photo showed a pair of starving children in Biafra, Africa, who were suffering horribly because of famine.[247] Disturbed by this tragedy, young Jobs went to see the pastor of the church where his parents had been taking him. He sincerely wanted to know why God allowed such tragedy in the world. But the pastor was dismissive of the budding genius and failed to provide an adequate answer. To this inquisitive soul, the pastor offered no reason to believe in the Gospel despite evil. Isaacson reports that Jobs announced that he no longer wanted to have anything to do with worshipping such a God again, and he never went back to church.[248] For the rest of his life, Steve Jobs desperately searched for the meaning of life, exploring Zen Buddhism and other confusing belief systems.[249] Even on his deathbed, witnesses state that he was grappling with the possibility of an afterlife.[250] Sadly, had that pastor done his homework and prepared himself to be ready to explain his hope as a believer, then who knows what kind of impact Steve Jobs would have made in this world beyond simply developing cutting-edge technology.

It seems that pain for many people calls into question their most fundamental beliefs about God. But can God really be blamed for the evil and suffering of the world? Is it God who is responsible? Furthermore, can one equate the presence of evil to the absence of God? That conclusion, once again, is quite a leap.

To blame God for the existence of evil is a display of intellectual arrogance. What is greater: the distance from a tiny ant's brain to the brilliant mind of Albert Einstein, or the distance from Albert Einstein's brain to the omniscient, infinite mind of God? Of course, the latter is true. Trying to comprehend with our feeble human minds why God would allow some short-range evil to produce a greater, long-range good would be more difficult than trying to explain the complex theory of general relativity to an insect.

An ancient man named Job encountered an unimaginable situation and came face to face with his theology of pain and suffering. After suddenly losing all of his family and assets and suffering a debilitating disease, he spent most of his memoir attempting to question God's motives. In chapters 38-40 of the book in the Old Testament with Job's namesake, God finally responded. He asked, "Where were you when I laid the foundations of the earth" (Job 38:4-7)? In other words, "Who do you think you are to question Me? You could not comprehend it even if I gave you an answer."

Would life not be wonderful without any pain? The Bible gives a clear response to those who might be tempted to blame God for the presence of evil and suffering. Let us follow along a sufficient line of reasoning from the Bible:

1. GOD CREATED THE WORLD GOOD.

Genesis 1:1, 31 In the beginning, God created the heavens and the earth... *(Then after creation week was completed)*, God looked over all He had made, and He saw that it was very good!

It was very good. When God created the world, there were no earthquakes, hurricanes, floods, droughts, diseases, adulteries, murders, crime, or death. Earth was an ideal paradise.

2. GOD CREATED PEOPLE WITH THE ABILITY TO CHOOSE.

> **Genesis 2:16-17** The Lord God warned the man, "You may freely eat the fruit of every tree in the garden—except the tree of the knowledge of good and evil. If you eat its fruit, then you are sure to die."

Being made in the image of God is what separates people from animals. Animals cannot make moral choices, but humans can. God gave people the power to choose. Why? Because choice is the essence of love. God is love and wants us to choose to love Him back. We are not inanimate objects.

Some ask why God created humanity if He knew that they would sin. Or they ask why God chose to create humanity with the ability to choose wrong. But if this arrangement were not the case, then we would no longer be relational; we would be machines—automatons. Imagine being married to a doll. Every morning when we woke up, we could merely pull its string, and it would be pre-programmed to say, "I love you." Though it would be a marriage without any conflict, there would be one major thing missing—a capacity for love. Who would want that scenario? Love is voluntary, but love is also risky. When a couple gets married, not only have they fallen in love, but they have also taken a risk—a risk that their spouse may not always make the best choices. But they each think it worth the risk and enter into matrimony anyway. Likewise, God thought we were worth the risk when He created us just the way we are.

3. PEOPLE CHOSE WRONGLY AND INTRODUCED EVIL INTO THE WORLD.

> **Genesis 3:6** [The woman] saw that the tree was beautiful, and its fruit looked delicious, and she wanted the wisdom it would give her. So, she took some of the fruit and ate it. Then she gave some to her husband, who was with her, and he ate it, too.

God gave Adam and Eve, the representatives of the entire human race, a choice of whether or not to abide by His direction. The freedom to choose also included having the freedom to choose wrongly. Unfortunately, they decided to disobey God by choosing evil. They chose wrongly.

> **Romans 5:12** When Adam sinned, sin entered the world. Adam's sin brought death, so death spread to everyone, for everyone sinned.

The evil and suffering in this world result from the free choices that people have exercised in the direction of evil. These choices were not just made by Adam and Eve, but by each one of us. When an individual attempts to blame God for the evil in the world, we need to gently point out to them that human beings are the ones who introduced evil, not God. So, He is not the One responsible. Sadly, people's anger towards God for evil has been grossly misdirected. God merely allowed evil to be possible, but people were the ones who made evil actual.[251]

4. THE PEOPLE'S WRONGFUL CHOICE HAD LASTING CONSEQUENCES.

> **Romans 8:20-22** Against its will, all creation was subjected to God's curse. But with eager hope, the creation looks forward to the day when it will join God's children in glorious freedom from death and decay. For we know that all creation has been groaning as in the pains of childbirth right up to the present time.

Due to all the evil that human beings introduced into God's perfect creation, the world is no longer good. We now live in a sin-cursed environment. Germs, erratic weather patterns, broken relationships, and locked doors to prevent crime are all consequences of sin. God's once beautiful paradise has been marred. The world is now defective, including every one of us. We are all born with a natural tendency toward self-destruction. The blame for evil and suffering lies at the feet of human irresponsibility, not God.

This fact, for example, can be seen in the issue of world hunger. While malnourished mothers hold their starving babies in many developing countries, what is the dominant theme of the best-selling books in developed countries? Dieting. And in some dense population centers, people worship their sources of food instead of eating them. In India, for instance, it is illegal to kill a cow for food due to their beliefs in reincarnation.[252] The truth is that the world produces enough food each day to give every person on the planet 3000 calories a day.[253] That amount of food fuel is not just enough to survive; it is actually enough to thrive. But the fact that the world's rich resources are unevenly distributed among the world's population is not God's fault. It is ingrained in our sinful nature to hoard and not share open handedly with those in need.

Some have asked, "Why does God not prevent terrorist attacks, child abuse, and other heinous crimes against humanity?" But the God who gives *us* a choice to either align with His principles or violate them is the same God who offers radical extremists and traffickers *their* choice. Like all of us, they choose to do evil. It is a worse evil, perhaps, but it is still evil all the same. If God blocked their choices, then He would also have to block our choices, too.[254] What kind of God would that be? God's commands are not designed to be legalistic and remove pleasure, but rather to protect humanity from the self-destructive tendencies that the sin nature in all of us causes. Any time we choose to violate God's commands, there is always a victim. Either we hurt ourselves or hurt others, but the result is always pain when we do wrong.

Given the four points above, we should not question why so many *bad* things happen to good people. Instead, we should wonder why so many *good* things happen to bad people.[255] Remember, no sin-prone person on the entire planet is considered good compared to God's holiness and moral perfection (Isaiah 64:6; Luke 18:19; Romans 3:10-12). God is full of grace and mercy; He gives us what we do not deserve (grace), and He does not give us what we do deserve (mercy).[256]

If God were to stamp out evil today, then He would do a complete job. We would all be wiped out. But we tend to be selective about His justice. While we may want Him to stop war, we also want Him to stay remote from us. But if God were to remove all evil from the universe, then His action would be complete and would have to include our lies and personal impurities, our lack of love, and our failure to do good as well. So, we should be relieved that God is gracious and allows some evil to continue to exist; otherwise, we would all be doomed immediately.[257] Thankfully, "the faithful love of the Lord never ends! His mercies never cease" (Lamentations 3:22).

Therefore, those who still insist that God could prevent suffering if He wanted to must come to terms with some logical absurdities. God can do anything because He is all-powerful. But He chooses to remain within the order of the universe that He already designed. So, there are some things that He will not do. For instance, God will not make a round square. He will also not make a rock so big that He cannot pick it up. Likewise, He will not make dry water. These examples are logical absurdities. In the same way, God will not give people free will on the one hand, and then, on the other hand, offer no possibility of moral evil and the suffering that follows it.[258] Once God chose to give free will to all human beings, then it was up to them, not God, as to whether or not they would sin and fall short of His expectations. Therefore, suffering cannot possibly be the result of a lack of divine love and power.

As has been said, for love to truly exist, there must be the presence of free will. But by the same token, the freedom to hate has to be a reality in a world where love is possible. A loving God gave us this world with its free agency, and then He also gave us strict instructions about how to operate in it—instructions on how to make the right choices for the greatest mutual benefit. Some people refuse to read the instructions and abide by them. But that is not because God is not loving; people choose wrongly to reject His teachings and do evil.

But here is a perplexing question: Why would anyone call a crime committed against someone else evil in the first place? In a postmodern world, is evil not a matter of personal opinion? Otherwise, we could make all evil go away by just changing our opinion. No, when someone commits a crime against someone else, then it is objectively and transcendently evil. But how could that be true

The Value Of Pain And Suffering

unless there is an objective, transcendent standard of righteousness by which we measure those crimes?

So, just as a crooked line can only be considered crooked when compared to a straight line, evil demonstrates the existence of a moral standard.[259] Inherently, we know this fact to be a reality. But from where did that moral standard come? It had to come from an objective, transcendent God. Hence, the presence of evil proves the existence of God. Since life is eternal, then whatever evil occurs here in our short ninety-year lifespan is negligible in comparison. But God often allows us to suffer something now so that we can have a better tomorrow (in eternity). The scope of eternity changes everything about the perspective of pain, suffering, and evil in this relatively brief life.[260]

5. THERE IS GOOD NEWS, THOUGH! LONG BEFORE PEOPLE EVER MADE THE WRONG DECISION, GOD HAD ALREADY DEVISED A BACK-UP PLAN.

1 Peter 1:19-20 It was the precious blood of Christ, the sinless, spotless Lamb of God. God chose Him as your ransom long before the world began, but now in these last days, He has been revealed for your sake.

Although God knew that people would sin, rather than refraining from creating them, He had already ordained and set in motion His great plan of salvation. When people sinned, if God had just sat back and said, "It is your fault; I will let you get what you deserve," then He would have been perfectly justified in doing so. Instead, He took all the suffering upon Himself because of His unfathomable love for us.

Isaiah 53:3-5 He was despised and rejected—a man of sorrows, acquainted with deepest grief... Yet it was our weaknesses He carried; it was our sorrows that weighed Him down. But He was pierced for our rebellion, crushed for our sins.

If God stayed in heaven and left us to grovel in our pain and try to find our way to heaven, then He would be justified in doing so. However, He went beyond all expectations and played by His own

133

rules. He is well acquainted with pain and suffering because He has experienced it first-hand. Because God came and entered our condition and became sin for us that we might become righteous, then there is certainly reason to believe that God is indeed a good God. He is undeniably both powerful and loving. Not only was He *willing* to provide a remedy for our hopeless situation, but He was also *capable* of providing it as well. So, God is, in fact, all-loving and all-powerful.

At the Cross, we see the absolute uniqueness of the Christian response to suffering. In Islam, however, the idea of God suffering is nonsense—it is thought to make God weak. And in Buddhism, to reach divinity is precisely to move beyond the possibility of suffering. But only in Christ do we have a God who is loving enough to suffer right along with us. The loving parent is not the one who never allows suffering in a child's life. Rather, the loving parent is the one who is willing to suffer alongside their children. And in Christianity, this profound truth is exactly what we find.[261]

6. THIS SIN-WRACKED WORLD IS VERY TEMPORARY.

2 Peter 3:9 The Lord isn't really being slow about His promise, as some people think. No, he is being patient for your sake. He does not want anyone to be destroyed but wants everyone to repent.

As we have just seen, we must not view the presence of pain and suffering as God being incapable or unwilling to eradicate it. The Bible promises that God will indeed deal with it once and for all, and He will do so very soon. But right now, He is patiently delaying His judgment so that more people will have time to turn to Him. So, instead of blaming God, we should be grateful to Him. It is just a matter of having some perspective adjustment.

Revelation 21:4 [God] will wipe every tear from their eyes, and there will be no more death or sorrow or crying or pain. All these things are gone forever.

Those who have accepted Christ as their personal Lord and Savior have a hope that sustains them despite whatever pain and suffering come their way.

The consummation of all things is soon to come, and all things will be made new. The paradise lost in Genesis will become the paradise found in Revelation.[262] In light of eternity, this parenthetical experience called "life on earth" is very brief. Compared to a lifetime, it would be like walking into a dingy hotel room for a few minutes and then deciding not to stay.

For those who decide against a relationship with Jesus, then He will grant them what they desire—separation from Him. However, that decision will not only last for the rest of one's life here on earth, but it will also last throughout eternity as well. There is also a place of eternal separation from God (Matthew 18:6-9; 25:31-46; Mark 9:42-48; 2 Thessalonians 1:5-10; Jude 7, 13; Revelation 14:9-11; Revelation 20:10, 14-15).

> **Ezekiel 33:11** As surely as I live, says the Sovereign Lord, I take no pleasure in the death of wicked people. I only want them to turn from their wicked ways so they can live.

> **Revelation 21:8** But cowards, unbelievers, the corrupt, murderers, the immoral, those who practice witchcraft, idol worshipers, and all liars—their fate is in the fiery lake of burning sulfur. This is the second death.

7. PAIN IS ACTUALLY A GIFT BECAUSE IT COMPELS US TO MAKE ALTERATIONS TO OUR LIFESTYLE.

> **Hebrews 12:7,8,9,11** As you endure this divine discipline, remember that God is treating you as His own children. Who ever heard of a child who is never disciplined by its father? Since we respected our earthly fathers who disciplined us, shouldn't we submit even more to the discipline of the Father of our spirits, and live forever? No discipline is enjoyable while it is happening—it's painful! But afterward there will be a peaceful harvest of right living for those who are trained in this way.

God will sometimes allow something difficult to occur for the greater good to come forth. It is not God's intention to make us happy, but to make us holy.[263] And sometimes, for us to become more like Him, His best tool is to allow a bit of pain. It is called "redemptive affliction."[264]

C.S. Lewis famously wrote, "We can ignore even pleasure. But pain insists upon being attended to. God whispers to us in our pleasures, speaks in our conscience, but shouts in our pains: it is His megaphone to rouse a deaf world."[265]

Suppose parents do not want their children to grow up to become spoiled and undisciplined. In that case, they have to apply some "redemptive affliction" from time to time during their children's formative years so that they modify their bad behavior into better behavior (Proverbs 13:24). Those parents have to inflict a very temporary bad experience so that some greater good will ultimately come forth permanently. This practice should flow out of parents' love for their children, not because of anger or annoyance.

But despite the explanation above, would life still not be better without pain? A pain-free life seems so attractive. Well, remarkably, there are a few places in the world where there is no physical pain. And it would be insightful to consider that context. Let us visit a leper colony.

People with leprosy do not feel any physical pain in certain parts of their bodies. But this peculiarity is actually the tragedy of their disease. As the sickness spreads, the nerve endings that carry pain signals grow silent. If a healthy person accidentally touches a hot stove burner, then they would instantly jerk away to prevent further damage and devote their time and resources to nursing their burn back to health as their highest priority. Their pain would demand an immediate response and command their attention. However, a leper would be unaware of the burn, so their tissue would continue to suffer damage beyond repair as it got severely injured and then goes untreated.[266]

For lepers, the absence of pain sensations results in unsightly deformities on the hands, feet, and face. Factors in the environment continue to damage the tissues in the body, but the victim remains unaware and fails to make any protective adjustments. Imagine an individual going blind because their eyes fail to signal them that they are too dry and need to blink. Or imagine one losing a thumb simply because they gripped a broomstick incorrectly. Leprosy is a cruel disease; there is no one in the world any lonelier than a leper. Their deformities often disgust the general population, which is fearful of catching the virus. Severe emotional pain is also a consequence of a leper's distance from pain. So, if one genuinely wants to know what a pain-free world would look like, then they can find the answer by visiting a leper colony. However, the victims there would be the first to insist that pain is actually a gift.

APPLICATION

What has your pain done for you? We may never know all the reasons why God permits pain, but like Job, we must trust in the sovereignty of God. We must allow it to make us better, not bitter.[267]

Horatio Spafford, a successful 19th-century lawyer, lost all he had in the great Chicago Fire in 1871. Then, after putting his family on a ship to Europe while he rebuilt their livelihood, he experienced tremendous loss when the ship sank and all four of his precious daughters drowned; only his wife survived. But out of this unfathomable grief, he wrote the famous hymn that revealed such a healthy perspective—*It is Well with My Soul*.[268] Later, Spafford abandoned his law practice and moved to Jerusalem to start a ministry reaching out to Jews living under Arab oppression in Palestine.[269] So out of Horatio's pain, his life was redirected, and he established a lasting legacy. His life efforts did not just end with his death; they far outlived him.

Most of us can look back on our lives and identify some moments of suffering that brought us closer to God than before. With time and perspective, most of us can see some good reasons for at least some of the tragedy and pain that God has allowed to occur in our lives.

We have to keep in mind that God will always redeem what He allows.[270] Because God is sovereign, then everything that happens

He must have allowed (Matthew 10:29). But because God is also love, He must want only what is best for us (1 John 4:8). Therefore, God redeems for the greater good all that He allows. Job's end was more than twice as much as when he was first introduced (Job 42:10-17). Though we may not always see or understand God's redemptive ways while we are here in this life, someday soon, we will (1 Corinthians 13:12). In the meantime, we can find solace in the beautiful reminder that "God causes everything to work together for the good of those who love God and are called according to His purpose for them" (Romans 8:28).

A corollary to the question of pain and suffering is another question that seems to cause a hurdle for some people: "Why would a loving God send people to hell?" That question is certainly valid, and we can begin to answer it by observing civic law. Suppose a prosecuting attorney neglects to seek justice for a victim's family by convicting their perpetrator and sending him to prison. In that case, he or she is doing further harm to the victim's family. How loving is it for those who do wrong to be treated the same way as those who do right? To be "loving" to the offender is to be unloving to the offended. The symbol of justice is a set of scales that are in balance. Likewise, in the end, there must be a balance between the love of God and the justice of God. The love of God necessitates the judgment of God. Logically, we cannot have one without the other.

Furthermore, God honors the wishes of people here on earth. There are millions of people who want no relationship with God. And their idea of a blissful eternity does not have God as a part of that picture. So, for those who have spent their entire life rejecting Him, then God is not going to force them into His presence for eternity. God loves us enough to allow us to make our own choice. But we just have to recognize that our choice has a consequence.

God has done all that He can do to convince us to spend eternity in His presence. He inspired writers of the Bible to instruct us. Then He sent His only Son to provide the way for us. And the Holy Spirit today pursues us and attempts to draw us to God. But for those who still choose to reject His presence after all of His overtures, then He allows them to do so. However, a place where God's presence is absent is a horrible place—a place of perpetual torment. Rest assured, God does not send anyone there, but people may choose to go there by their own choice. An apologist is responsible for making sure that people understand their choices and the benefits or consequences of those choices.

CHAPTER 8

THE COMPARISON OF CHRISTIANITY TO OTHER WORLD RELIGIONS

KEY SCRIPTURES

John 14:6 Jesus told him, "I am the way, the truth, and the life. No one can come to the Father except through Me."

Ephesians 2:8-9 God saved you by His grace when you believed. And you can't take credit for this; it is a gift from God. Salvation is not a reward for the good things we have done, so none of us can boast about it.

2 Corinthians 5:19-20 For God was in Christ, reconciling the world to Himself, no longer counting people's sins against them. And He gave us this wonderful message of reconciliation. So we are Christ's ambassadors; God is making His appeal through us. We speak for Christ when we plead, "Come back to God!"

WORLD RELIGIONS AND APOLOGETICS

"Deep in the heart of every person is a God-shaped vacuum that only He can fill." Although this statement is often erroneously attributed to Blaise Pascal, it is still profoundly true.[271] Suffice to say, every person in every culture is in search of life's ultimate meaning. They are also acutely aware of their failings. So in an attempt to answer the overarching questions of life, and out of people's need to improve themselves, religions emerge. People have various forms of faith, and these forms take on different institutions and practices that become sacred to the masses in the multiple cultures that observe them. Interestingly, most of these worldviews are merely reflections of the people who observe them, as if a mirror was put in the sky reflecting those below. The aspirations, fears, hopes, and desires of a people group will often shape their belief system, reinforcing their faith in their own worldview.

According to some estimates, there are roughly 4,200 religions, churches, and faith groups worldwide. Since boutique postmodernism encourages individuals to craft a unique religious worldview suited to themselves, one might count as many as seven billion religions in the world. However, in this chapter, only five major world religions will be explored—Islam, Hinduism, Buddhism, Atheism, and Christianity.

Why study the religions of the world as a part of apologetics? Dynamics have shaped European thought over the past several millennia, from Greek and Roman culture, the Middle Ages, Renaissance, and World Discovery to the Protestant Reformation, Age of Enlightenment, Imperialism, Industrial Revolution, and the Digital Age. This cumulative European worldview has shaped American thought today. In an ever-changing world, apologists have had to continually adapt their message to continue their vigilant defense of Christianity.

However, the twenty-first century has brought about a "shrinking of the world" due to globalization. Significant factors are at play, such as mass global communications, affordable international transportation, trade, and shared technology. Now, millennials in the West interact with those from Eastern persuasions frequently and freely.

So, apologists not only have to be aware of how Western secularists feel and think, but they also have to be mindful of how Eastern religious people feel and think, too. When antagonism and opposition against Christianity come from multiple fronts, then those explaining and defending Christianity must understand a wide range of conflicting worldviews and equip themselves with various responses to maintain effectiveness in fulfilling the Great Commission. Thus, a healthy understanding of world religions is a necessary part of 21st-century apologetics. How do the claims of Jesus compare to the central tenets of other popular religions?

THE COHERENCE AND CONSISTENCY OF CHRISTIANITY

A worldview is not built on merely one line of an argument. Rather, a worldview is built upon a connected series of arguments. As has been a premise throughout this book, four main questions provide the foundation upon which a worldview is built—*Where did I come from?* (origin), *Why am I here?* (purpose), *How should I behave?* (morality), and *Where am I ultimately going?* (destiny). The answers to these four questions provide the meaning of life for every single member of the human race.[272] Every person on the planet is eventually confronted by them and searches for answers to them, whether consciously or unconsciously.

Additionally, there are three tests for truth—logical consistency, empirical adequacy, and experiential relevance.[273] So, there are three tests for four questions. Therefore, for a worldview to be true, the thread of answers to all four questions must satisfy all three tests and be coherent and void of any contradictions.

Only one Founder of a religion was ever able to sufficiently provide the answers to all four of those questions in such a narrow way that corresponded with reality. There is coherence among the answers that Jesus provided, unlike those of any other religion.[274] For instance, as we will see later in this chapter, in Buddhism, the basis for origins creates problems for the basis of morality. And regarding Hinduism, Gandhi himself admitted that he would have liked to expunge some of the scriptures from the *Vedas* because they were so conflicting. In Islam, there are undeniable contradictions between the early and later portions of the *Qur'an* as well as the claims and lifestyle of Mohammed. This challenge plagues mullahs to this day and contentiously divides Sunnis from Shi'ites worldwide. In contrast, Christianity is one complete system; it answers all four questions with total coherence and absolute consistency. And it also satisfies the rigors of all three tests. So, the soundness of the Gospel strongly suggests that it is true.

When one considers the fulfilled prophecies about Jesus, the purity of His life, the uniqueness of His death, and the miracle of His resurrection, what else would one need to prove His deity? He did prove it, soundly. And all four questions are also answered correspondingly with truth, and they are all coherent when put together.[275]

Contrary to the popular notion today, all religions are not the same. Some claim that all world religions are fundamentally the same and only superficially different, but in reality, they are fundamentally different and superficially similar.[276] Every worldview cannot lead to the same God. Why? Because each major world religion claims exclusivity, not just Christianity. When something is known to be true, then it necessarily excludes all other suggestions. 2+2 cannot be 3; it is exclusively 4.

Hinduism is exclusive. In fact, it is so exclusive that if one decides to marry a non-Hindu, then they risk being disowned by the rest of the family. Buddhism also rejects all other worldviews. Non-Buddhists are forced to flee Southeast Asian countries like Myanmar and Cambodia in search of religious freedom, or else they suffer severe discrimination. And Islam is so hostile to other beliefs that if a Muslim dares to convert to another religion, then they are considered an apostate and are condemned to death, even by their own family members. Atheism is exclusive. While it claims to be the champion of tolerance, it is extremely intolerant of those who have faith in Jesus. Truth, by definition, is exclusive.

But the difference in Christianity from all other world religions is that while it is exclusive—Jesus is the only way to reconciliation with God—it is also inclusive. It is not limited to a particular caste or to one who has achieved certain standards. No, one of the foundation stones of Christianity is that it is open and free to everyone. "For everyone who calls on the name of the Lord will be saved" (Romans 10:13). So, in the person of Jesus, Christianity is true because it coheres all the questions with the tests for truth. Likewise, Jesus distinguishes Himself from all other religious leaders because all of His answers correspond together.

Furthermore, all roads cannot lead to God because the different worldviews make contradictory claims, especially regarding the Person of Jesus and our ability to relate with God. For instance, Islam claims that Jesus was just a good teacher, but not God. Christianity, however, claims that Jesus was both a good teacher as well as God. Both of those views—the Muslim view and the Christian view—can be false or one can be true, but both cannot be true because they make contradictory claims. The claims of the Christian view are unique—Jesus rose from the grave. This claim distinguishes Christianity from all other religions. Islam does not claim that Mohammed rose from the dead. Buddhism does not claim that Buddha came back from the grave. Only Christianity claims that Jesus resurrected from the dead, a view that, as we have seen, can be substantiated by careful examination and has already proved His deity. Jesus is the only way to God because He *is* God, a path that is very different from all others.[277] In fact, all other roads not only contradict the only narrow path that leads to God, but they also all lead to disappointing dead ends.

BRIEF OVERVIEW OF WORLD RELIGIONS AND HOW TO SHARE THE GOSPEL

Hinduism

The Hindu religion originated over 3000 years ago in India and comprises over 900 million people today. Their sacred texts are *The Vedas, Upanishads, Bhagavad Gita,* and *Ramayana.* While Hinduism has no official doctrinal statement, it has a core of shared beliefs that revolve around the impersonal nature of the universe and the impact that it should have on humanity. Its doctrine claims that Brahman is the supreme but impersonal god, and that all other gods (330 million of them) are extensions of this ultimate deity.

It teaches that the entire universe, including people on earth, are extensions of this god. A person's ultimate goal of existence is to lose themselves and become one with Brahman over time, a state called enlightenment.[278]

Christians can connect with Hindus on the fact that both religions emphasize the importance of the spiritual realm, believe that Jesus existed, and desire to please their gods and seek salvation in the afterlife.

Hinduism also claims exclusivity—that it is the only true religion. Its beliefs affect every part of its followers' lives, including how they spend their time, what they eat, and the people with whom they associate. However, Hinduism teaches that everyone is trapped in a cycle of reincarnation and karma, meaning that upon death, an individual is "born again" as a plant, animal, another person, or oneness with their god, depending upon how good they were in their previous life.

It also promotes that there are three ways to either break or improve this cycle. The first way is the "way of works," one's attempt to purify their soul by careful obedience to the obligations stipulated in the Hindu *Vedas*. The second way is the "way of knowledge," one's complete rejection of their life and their mystical realization of identity with Brahman. And the third and most popular way is the "way of devotion," one's total commitment to the worship of their god in hopes that that particular deity will release them from, or advance them in, the reincarnation cycle and bring them into oneness with their god. The result of each is a state of utter bliss in union with their god, or as they say, a state of enlightenment.[279]

In their attempts to reach Hindus, Christians should keep in mind that they come from a radically different way of looking at the world. Because Hindus vary in their perspectives as wide or wider than Christians, they do not all believe the same thing. Therefore, an apologist should begin by listening intently to their particular view to understand from where they are coming, specifically understanding which of the three ways to salvation they have chosen.

From there, a believer can tailor their witnessing efforts accordingly. Of course, terms mean different things, so a Christian must define God, salvation, and heaven clearly. One must not forget to emphasize that Jesus is the only way to heaven because of His grace upon our faith, which should be refreshing because it is not by way of works, knowledge, and devotion of which Hindus are familiar.

Lastly, since peace is so elusive for a Hindu because of the endless cycle of death and rebirth, then a Christian can offer this peace as a benefit of total surrender to Jesus. A key verse to keep in mind when witnessing to a Hindu is the soothing message of Jesus: "Come to Me, all of you who are weary and carry heavy burdens, and I will give you rest" (Matthew 11:28). Of course, sharing one's testimony of gaining a personal relationship with the one, true, personal God is very effective, too.

Provocative questions to ask a Hindu for meaningful conversation:

- What parts of Hinduism are difficult for you?

- Do you believe that all religions lead to God?

- What do you think happens after we die?

- What is your opinion about Jesus Christ?

- Do you think there is a difference between a religion and a relationship with God?

Buddhism

The Buddhist religion originated in Northeast India and eventually spread throughout Southeast Asia, comprising about 600 million adherents. Its sacred texts are the *Tripitaka* and the Mahayana sutras, and was founded by Siddhartha Gautama about 550 years before Christ.[280] Born in a privileged and affluent household, Gautama traveled the world and was troubled by all the hardship and suffering of the common people. So, to identify with them, Gautama chose to become a homeless beggar. He found that the Hindu scriptures and priests were not helpful to him and what he wanted to achieve in life, so he charted a different course of beliefs. He practiced self-denial and meditation, believing that it would lead to peace and the relief of suffering. The ultimate goal of his new religion was to achieve a god-like state of Nirvana. As he traveled to spread his message far and wide, he became known as "the enlightened one," or the "Buddha."

Christians can connect with Buddhists on their shared desire for peace and being in tune with their inner selves. Although Buddhists believe that Jesus existed as a good teacher, they think of Him as being less important than Buddha. While both Christians and Buddhists believe in life after death, Buddhists are best known for their concerns about evil, suffering, and the conflict in the world.

Buddhists acknowledge that the Buddha never claimed to be a god. Rather, he considered himself one who showed "the way" to enlightenment for others. So, Buddhists do not worship Buddha. Instead, they revere him as a great teacher. They also believe in the Four Noble Truths: 1) pain and suffering exist in the world, 2) an attachment to people and things contributes to that suffering, 3) suffering stops only after a person can rid themselves of all desires, and 4) there is a path that will extinguish all of our desires.[281]

Buddhists believe in reincarnation, albeit differently from Hindus. They believe in reincarnation through the cycles of karma. Driven by a law of cause and effect, they believe that whatever they do in their lifetime, either good or bad, determines what will happen to them in the next lifetime. This cycle continues until they endure enough pain and suffering to be purified enough to reach Nirvana, a state characterized by freedom from pain, worry, and the external world. Like Hindus, Buddhists believe that salvation is by self-effort through the Four Noble Truths, and is only realized once one is finally free from the cycle of karma.

Because there are so many varying perspectives in the Buddhist religion, Christians need to listen to an individual's worldview and seek to understand where they are coming from specifically. The key is pointing to the possibility through Jesus of the endless freedom from suffering, guilt, and sin because of the gift of eternal life in heaven. Of course, terms mean different things, so a Christian should avoid using terms like "born again" without defining them clearly. And because Buddhists believe that salvation is achieved through self-effort and as a result of cause and effect, one must not forget to emphasize that Jesus offers eternal life by grace through faith alone.

Lastly, Christians should emphasize the uniqueness of Jesus. He conquered death and evil by rising from the dead. He alone will either alleviate one's suffering or provide the supernatural grace to endure it. A key verse to keep in mind when witnessing to a Buddhist is the refreshing relief of true salvation: "God saved you by His grace when you believed. And you cannot take credit for this; it is a gift from God. Salvation is not a reward for the good things we have done, so none of us can boast about it" (Ephesians 2:8-9). It is also very effective to share one's own story of gaining a personal relationship with the one true God. Amid our suffering, we can be free from guilt and have an assurance of eternal life.

Provocative questions to ask a Buddhist for meaningful conversation:

- What parts of Buddhism are you most excited about?

- Why do you think there is evil and suffering in the world?

- What do you think happens after we die?

- Who or what set the laws of karma in motion?

- Have you ever felt the need to be forgiven?

- How would you feel if you discovered that someone else suffered in your place so that you would not have to suffer eternally?

- Have you ever heard of a path to inner peace apart from ridding yourself of all your desires and attachments?

Islam

Those who call themselves Muslims belong to the religion called Islam. Islam means "the way of submission." Their beliefs are based on their scriptures, the *Qur'an*, and their traditions, the *Hadith*. Their founder, Mohammed, claimed that the angel Gabriel dictated the *Qur'an* to him beginning in 622 A.D. in Saudi Arabia. This religion has grown to become the second-largest religion globally after Christianity, claiming 1.3 billion followers, primarily in the Middle East among Arab and Persian countries between the 10th and 40th parallels on a globe. Muslims faithfully gather on Fridays in their places of worship called mosques to pray to Allah. When praying, whether in a mosque or elsewhere, they always face east toward Mecca, the birthplace of Islam, where Mohammed had his vision.[282]

Christians can connect with Muslims on several points. Islam is one of the few monotheistic religions of the world; its followers believe in one god, Allah. They also have a commitment to prayer and living a devoted life that is pleasing to their god. They believe in a similar afterlife, paradise and hell. But because they only believe that Jesus was a prophet who was inferior to Mohammed, was not the Son of God, and who did not die for the sins of the world, then they have no chance of really being saved while remaining strictly in their belief system.

Like those of most other religions, subscribers to Islam believe that their faith is the only true religion. At the core of Islam, there are seven fundamental beliefs that every Muslim must accept:

1. Allah

2. The angels (both good and evil)

3. The revealed books of Allah

4. Allah's many prophets—Adam, Abraham, Moses, David, and Mohammed

5. The Last Day or Final Judgment

6. Belief in the divine measurement of human affairs

7. Belief in life after death[283]

These beliefs affect every part of a Muslim's life, including how they spend their time, what they eat, and even the types of friends they choose.

Sadly, they believe only a part of the Bible, and even their versions of that portion are badly corrupted and inaccurate. If a Muslim is faithful, then they believe that they will be rewarded for their faithfulness in eternal paradise. However, for infidels (those who do not believe in and submit to Allah), they will suffer for eternity in hell. They believe in salvation, but that it is only achieved through absolute obedience to Allah, the *Qur'an*, and the Five Pillars of Islam.

The Five Pillars are:

1. Affirmation (consistent recitation of the creed "There is no god but Allah, and Mohammed is his messenger")

2. Prayer (praying toward Mecca five times a day)

3. Alms (giving 2.5% of their income to the poor)

4. Fasting (abstaining from food and other indulgences from dawn to dusk every day during Ramadan)

5. Pilgrimage (visiting Mecca at least once in their lifetime)[284]

As with all other major world religions, Muslims can vary significantly in their perspectives. So, understanding is critical when a Christian builds a bridge to connect with a follower of the Islamic faith. Developing a genuine friendship and allowing them to know what a true Christian is really like is a powerful testimony. Since their culture and religion emphasize hospitality, a personal invitation into one's home is of great value, as long as one is careful to respect their dietary restrictions. Christians must be sensitive that the Islamic faith is inseparably tied to their family and culture. If a Muslim converts to become a follower of Jesus, then their family and friends will reject them, and in some cases, even seek to have them killed. So, a Christian must be patient while a Muslim considers all the consequences of placing their complete trust in Christ. One must keep in mind that there is a small sliver of common ground—they do acknowledge Jesus and the Bible, although neither are considered sacred. However, a Christian should emphasize the deity of Jesus and the divine inspiration of the Bible. Islam and Christianity differ radically because Islam views Allah as a god of anger and demand. There is no grace and mercy in Islam. Again, one's own story of gaining a personal relationship with the one true personal God will go a long way, and an emphasis upon the love and unconditional forgiveness of God will be refreshing to a Muslim.

Provocative questions to ask a Muslim for meaningful conversation:

- What are the most interesting parts of the Muslim religion?

- Do you follow Islam by your own choice, or because it is your family's tradition?

- Why is entrance into heaven based on living The Five Pillars of Islam?

- What do you think about Jesus Christ?

- Is it possible that Jesus could have been the Son of God?

Atheism

Atheism is defined as "not having a 'god belief.'" This worldview is about as old as humanity itself, but ancient Greek philosophers quantified its tenets into a systematic belief system. Then throughout the Enlightenment Era of the 18th century, more philosophers finetuned the atheist worldview even further. Influential works that shaped atheist thought include those by Marx, Freud, Feuerbach, and Voltaire, and notable modern authors include Richard Dawkins and Carl Sagan. This worldview is driven by pure rationality, reason, and the scientific method. It rejects the possibility of the spiritual world, the supernatural, divine intervention, and an afterlife. Those holding to these views comprise a little over a billion people in the world today.[285]

Christians can connect with Atheists on their shared commitment to reason and logic. God is committed to reason and logic as well. And since atheists seem to relish in the tough questions, Christians should feel comfortable asking probing ones that will create some doubt in their faulty worldview. God is bigger than any question. Atheists also believe that no one has all the answers, so chances are, the atheist with whom a Christian is conversing should be open to discovering facts outside their understanding. Furthermore, an atheist has faced a lifetime of hurts and hardships like the rest of us, but without having the peace of God to help them through those challenging situations. And since God created all humanity with "eternity in their hearts" (Ecclesiastes 3:11), a Christian is best poised to discuss the concerns in an atheist's heart about the afterlife. Remember, they, too, must eventually answer the four fundamental questions of life.

Atheists believe that their ideas spring from the most rational and reasonable worldview. And since they view religion as an unnecessary shackle upon people, of course, they believe their worldview is the only way. When observing the world according to the scientific method, it seems to be the most consistent with that approach. However, most atheists try to force their observations into the very narrow category of empirical science (observable and repeatable present processes) instead of considering observations and clues in the much broader category of forensic science (unobservable and unrepeatable past processes). Furthermore, atheists often point to negative situations caused by religion throughout the centuries (sexual suppression, ostracization of aberrant communities, oppression of minorities, ignoring physical abuse, wars and ethnic cleansing, violence by fundamentalists, intolerance, opposition to progress, superstition, etc.).

Regarding Jesus, most atheists acknowledge that He was a historical figure—even a good teacher and a moral person—but that He was not extraordinary enough to be God because, in their worldview, there is no reality beyond the human experience. To an atheist, the Bible is merely a collection of myths, half-truths, and lies designed to lead ignorant people astray and give power over the masses to religious leaders. They do not believe in an afterlife; people simply die and go back to the dust from which they came. To them, there is no eternal spirit in a person, nor heaven and hell. Therefore, for an atheist, there is no need for salvation from sin and hell. If sin and hell do not exist, then why would anyone need to be saved? From their humanistic perspective, despite any challenges that may arise, one does not need to run to an imaginary God; humanity has all it needs to solve all its problems.[286]

In their attempts to reach atheists, Christians should ask if they really seek to discover the truth, even if it costs them their reputation. If they are interested, then the other chapters in this book will certainly help them explore wherever the evidence leads with an open mind. But if they are not interested in genuinely seeking the essence of reality, then it will be difficult to have an honest and meaningful discussion. Only prayer will result in the spiritual impact that is needed.

The key to unlocking an atheist's mind and heart is to avoid futile arguments about what God has or has not done. Instead, one should focus on the evidence that Jesus was who He said He was and did what He claimed to do—that He is God, died on the Cross for a reason, and resurrected from the dead. Discussions about morality are not helpful, either, since sin is not an issue with an atheist. How can one break the universal laws of God if He does not even exist?

As with any other worldview, Christians cannot argue an atheist into faith in Christ. Rather, a more effective approach is to be their friend and exemplify such an attractive Christ-like lifestyle that they sense something different and something they need, especially when they encounter a crisis and they lose control of the factors in life. Lastly, it is crucial to remember the power in sharing one's own story of being transformed by a living God through faith in Jesus.

Provocative questions to ask an atheist for meaningful conversation:

- Do you ever feel judged by others for rejecting the existence of God?

- What led you to choose to not believe in the existence of God?

- Are you willing to exercise academic integrity and go wherever the evidence leads?

- Since some scientists have concluded that evidence like specified complexity in a fine-tuned universe points to an intelligent designer, then is it theoretically possible that there is intentional design behind our world?

- Have you ever considered the possibility that you could be wrong about the existence of God? What might be the consequences if you happen to be wrong?

CONCLUSION

As one can see from the review of the world's major religions, each one tends to reduce spirituality down to a moralizing, self-determining, and works-oriented expression. In Buddhism, for instance, one must work their way into Nirvana. In Islam, no matter how hard one strives, it is still up to the will of Allah as to whether or not he grants a person access to paradise. And in Hinduism, one is on their own in an attempt to gain release from karma. So, if they are not careful, Christians can fall into this trap as well, especially if their focus is on outer piety rather than an inward relationship with Jesus.

This striving for spiritual perfection was not the intent of God when He created the human race. The Christian faith is the only faith that bridges what *should* be and what *can* be by the grace of God. When Jesus was asked what the greatest law is, He condensed 613 laws given by Moses into just two—love God with one's whole being and love one's neighbor as oneself. These two commands were never intended to be disconnected.

When one reads the *Vedas, Upanishads,* and the *Bhagavad Gita* of Hinduism, the *Qur'an* and *Hadith* of Islam, and the *Tripitaka* and *Sutras* of Buddhism, they will find that they are each interesting in their own way. The authors present attractive ideas, even wisdom. By sheer common sense, most of these religious books agree with each other on certain points of morality. But when all the other sacred writings of the world are compared to the Bible, several crucial things are missing:

1. None claim to be the revelation of God Himself to people. None speak as if God is reaching down to people to show them how to have a relationship with Himself. Rather, according to them, if we are ever to reach a Higher Power, it will have to be the result of sheer human effort.

2. They are each merely a list of rules and regulations—a challenge to outer piety. There are no themes of love, grace, mercy, forgiveness, or a divine relationship.

3. Regarding the four basic questions of life that provide meaning—*where did we come from?* (origins), *why are we here?* (purpose), *how should we behave?* (morality), and *where are we going?* (destiny)—all other sacred writings either contradict themselves or avoid some of these questions altogether. Coherence and consistency fall short when the sacred writings of their worldviews are put to the test.

On the other hand, the Bible is unique in that, while it does contain instructions on proper living, the predominant theme is God's initiative to reconcile humanity unto Himself. While there are some ceremonial laws mingled in with the moral laws in the Old Testament, these two categories of all the commandments are easily distinguished from each other. It is also common knowledge that Jesus fulfilled all the Old Testament ceremonial laws. So, while the Bible's moral instructions remain intact and should be followed today, the ceremonial laws do not have to be observed any longer.

The Bible's emphasis is all about divine relationship. It is a living communication from a personal God to each individual in the human race.[287] In fact, when Jesus encountered the Pharisees, He scolded those who demonstrated outer piety in the absence of divine relationship. Furthermore, regarding the four basic questions of life referenced above that we must all answer—origins, purpose, morality, and destiny—the Bible is the only sacred text that offers a clear, concise, coherent, and congruent set of answers.[288]

Not only does God exist, but He also speaks in a way that we can know Him. Knowing God and having a vibrant relationship with Him distinguishes the Christian faith from all other faiths. And it is what separates the Bible from all other sacred writings. While other religious texts can tell people how to behave, the Bible is God's revelation about how we can have a purposeful relationship with Him.

In today's world of tolerance, to declare that the Bible is right and that all the other writings are wrong sounds bigoted and socially unacceptable. But given a choice, it would be more prudent to be politically incorrect but logically correct. When choosing a book for spiritual guidance, it must be complete and correct in all aspects; otherwise, it could never significantly impact a person's life or be depended upon to help make important decisions.

When a Christian is sharing their faith with someone who has been influenced by one of the other world religions, it is important to remember that all other religions stress commitments to methods of self-improvement. This emphasis is seen in the Noble Eightfold Path of Buddhism, the Five Pillars of Islam, meditation, good works, or even the Ten Commandments of Judaism. While those means are clearly defined, they also become an arduous struggle for perfection.[289] In the end, such an ideal is elusive, it leaves one empty, and the Higher Power for whom they are desperately searching is still separated and distant (because it is non-existent). However, Christians must emphasize that Jesus is different. Our hope is not in following laws or standards, but in knowing Him who fully accepts us, not because of our works, but because of our faith in Him and our accepting His sacrifice for us.[290] It is not about what we have to do for God to merit our salvation; it is about what He has already done for us because of His loving grace and tender mercy. No other religion in the world offers an intimate relationship with God as a free gift. Summarily, while everyone else in the world is reaching up, God has already reached down through Jesus Christ.

The question is often posed, "If Christianity is true, then why are there so many different denominations?" For humans to hold any view about any subject, there is going to be variety. This diversity, however, tells us more about human nature than it does about the worldview itself. Atheism is also divided into many different camps. So is Islam. And so are Americans, Australians, Kiwanians, women, baseball fans, music enthusiasts, and every other people group. But this fact does not mean that Mohammed never existed, that a guitar is just a figment of our imagination, or that the existence of the United States of America should be questioned. The presence of varying views about a particular subject does not mean that it does not exist; quite the contrary. So, why should anyone be surprised that there exists a variety of views in Christianity? These varying views ultimately result from people's styles, personal preferences, and interpretations about certain truth statements in the Bible.[291]

Most importantly, beyond all the philosophical and propositional approaches that have been explored in the preceding chapters, the greatest apologetic is actually embedded in the gospel message itself. Every person on the planet yearns to be loved unconditionally; it is the way people are created. But as great as human love is, it can only go so far. Due to our frailties and shortcomings, no one can love and be loved perfectly. Yet, the longing for perfect love persists in all of us. The Gospel provides the only solution to the deepest desire of the human heart; God loves us unconditionally. Additionally, every human being is well aware of the mess that they have made in their lives. Our carnal, sin-prone nature drives us to be destructive; we end up hurting ourselves as well as those around us. Even those with high ideals often realize just how far they are living beneath those standards. But again, the Gospel addresses this condition. God, who loves unconditionally, is also willing to forgive all our transgressions. So, when we acknowledge our failure and reach out to God for assistance, then He is quite willing and able to restore order out of the chaos that we have created in our lives. This foundational message is the best apologetic.

Therefore, as Christians engaged in the work of defending and explaining the Gospel, we must never let the *work* of apologetics distract us from the *power* of apologetics already embedded in the Christan message.[292] 2 Corinthians 5:19-20 sums it up well: "For God was in Christ, reconciling the world to Himself, no longer counting people's sins against them. And He gave us this wonderful message of reconciliation. So, we are Christ's ambassadors; God is making His appeal through us."

CONCLUSION

Today, as in every generation before us, strident forces attempt to silence the Good News of Jesus' liberating power that is available to every human being on the planet. Although these powers exist in the unseen spiritual realm (Ephesians 6:12), they often manifest themselves covertly in a culture that is hostile to the Gospel. As early as the 1st-century Early Church, followers of Jesus have been disparaged and belittled because of their faith and firmly held convictions (1 Corinthians 1:18; Acts 4:13). Today is certainly no different. Yet, the hope that God provides those who follow Him is very attractive to a world that otherwise has no hope (Romans 15:13). One's hope is a distinguishing characteristic of a person of faith. So, from time to time, people who have never experienced the saving power of Jesus will inquire why a follower of Jesus has such consistent love, joy, peace, patience, kindness, goodness, faithfulness, gentleness, and self-control. In these divine appointments, one should be ready to explain their faith in Jesus and the hope that they have to an open inquirer (1 Peter 3:15), as well as be ready to defend their faith in Jesus to someone who is oppositional to the things of God (Jude 3). Because of this responsibility, apologetics is a sacred assignment for every devoted follower of Jesus. A Christian does not have to be intimidated by this mandate; Jesus has promised to be right there beside them whenever the occasion arises (Matthew 10:19-20; Luke 12:12; Luke 21:15). They just need to possess some courage.

We have seen that everyone has faith; everyone on the planet believes in ideas that they have not proven. We all trust that things we have been told are true. We have also seen that everyone has bias. Even the most conscientious scientists seem to allow their prejudices to taint their observations. People insist that what they believe is true simply because they have a prior philosophical commitment to believing so. In this book, then, we have had to weigh all the evidence of various views and evaluate which ones make the most sense, remembering that the wisest thing to do is to believe what requires the least amount of assumptions.

We have seen that the existence of God is the most rational idea, especially given the weak alternatives. We have also seen that since God is all-loving in His nature, then it is plausible that He would desire an object of His love. So, why would God not create an entire world as a context for His prized creation—people in His own image—so that they could respond to His love in an intimate relationship? And since God wanted to communicate with each individual of humanity how to have such a divine relationship, then we have seen that that communique would most likely look like the Bible. The evidence certainly suggests quite convincingly that the Bible is God-inspired. Furthermore, since God exists and desires a relationship with us, and since our wrong-doing has separated us from a holy God, then we have seen the need for reconciliation. God's mission to come as Jesus, take our place, pay the penalty of our sin, and reconcile us to Him makes logical sense. The evidence overwhelmingly suggests that Jesus is indeed God and that He came to earth to interact with the people of creation and to conquer death, hell, and the grave to reconcile humanity unto Himself.

So, why do so many people reject such a coherent set of ideas, especially in light of the inconsistency of all the other world religions and what they have to offer? Why is the Good News not considered so good? It is because of the sin nature with which every human being is born. Everyone seeks independence and self-sufficiency; it is our natural inclination. To admit that there is a God and His divine plan is to also admit that He is in charge and we are not. It is difficult for many people to surrender their autonomy and submit to the God described in the Bible, which results in indifference or hostility to these ideas. Sadly, in the rejection of God, the people of the world still attempt to fill the vacuum. And they do so by either secularism or mysticism; they either try to reject God outright or substitute Him for other higher powers.

However, because God is love and wants no one to spend eternity separated from Him (2 Peter 3:9), He sent messengers to communicate His message of reconciliation and preserve it in the Bible. He has also sent messengers to share His message of reconciliation with everyone on the planet. So, the study of apologetics is not reserved simply for theologians or pastors; it is the privilege and opportunity for every Christ-follower. We have been entrusted with the hope and truth that the world is so desperately craving. The reality that God is love and desires a relationship with each of us has to be shared convincingly and defended vigilantly.

Now, may God grant the reader the grace to share the faith, and when necessary, gently defend it with skill and love.

Endnotes

1   Ratio Christi, "What if Christianity is True?" April 11, 2020. https://ratiochristi.org/what-if-christianity-is-true-ebook/

2   Robehmed, Natalie. *Forbes,* "At 21, Kylie Jenner Becomes the Youngest Self-Made Billionaire Ever." March 5, 2019. https://www.forbes.com/sites/natalierobehmed/2019/03/05/at-21-kylie-jenner-becomes-the-youngest-self-made-billionaire-ever/#c6f8a112794a

3   Peterson-Withorn, Chase and Madeline Berg. Forbes, "Inside Kylie Jenner's Web of Lies—And why She's No Longer a Billionaire." March 29, 2020. https://www.forbes.com/sites/chasewithorn/2020/05/29/inside-kylie-jennerss-web-of-lies-and-why-shes-no-longer-a-billionaire/#75f3382425f7

4   ibid.

5   ibid. Editor's Updated Article, June 1, 2020.

6   Batts, Martin. "A Summary and Critique of the Historical Apologetic of John Warwick Montgomery." Th.M. Thesis, Dallas Theological Seminary, 1977. P. 1.

7   Root, Jerry. *Christianity Today,* "What are Christian Apologetics and How do they Relate to the Gospel Anyways?" June 14, 2018. https://www.christianitytoday.com/edstetzer/2018/june/what-are-christian-apologetics-and-how-do-they-relate-to-go.html

8   Beattie, Francis R. *Apologetics, Or, The Rational Vindication of Christianity* (Richmond, VA: Presbyterian Committee of Publication. 1903)

9   ibid.

10 Limbaugh, David. Forward to *I Don't Have Enough Faith to be an Atheist* by Norman Geisler and Frank Turek (Wheaton, IL: CrossWalk Books, 2004) 5.

11 Aune, David. "Justin Martyr's Use of The Old Testament." *Bulletin of the Evangelical Theological Society.* 1966.

12 Chadwick, Henry. *Early Christian Thought and the Classical Tradition: Studies In Justin, Clement, And Origen.* (Oxford, UK: Clarendon, 1966)

13 Trigg, Joseph Wilson. *The Bible and Philosophy In The Third Century.* (Atlanta, GA: John Knox Press, 1983)

14 Boa, Kenneth, and Robert Bowman, Jr. *Faith Has Its Reasons.* eBook, 2020. https://bible.org/series/faith-has-its-reasons.

15 John A., Mourant. "The Augustinian Argument for the Existence of God," *Inquiries Into Medieval Philosophy: A Collection In Honor Of Francis P. Clarke, Ed. James F. Ross (Contributions In Philosophy), Vol. 4.* (Westport, CT: Greenwood Publishing, 1971)

16 Boa, Kenneth, and Robert Bowman, Jr. *Faith Has Its Reasons.* eBook, 2020. https://bible.org/series/faith-has-its-reasons.

17 Harvard University, Religious Literacy Project, "The Protestant Movement." https://rlp.hds.harvard.edu/religions/christianity/protestant-movement

18 Pascal, Blaise, and W. F. Trotter. *Pascal's Pensées* (London, UK: J.M. Dent & Sons, 1931)

19 Boa, Kenneth, and Robert Bowman, Jr. *Faith Has Its Reasons.* eBook, 2020. https://bible.org/series/faith-has-its-reasons.

20 Newman, Barclay Moon. *A Concise Greek-English Dictionary of the New Testament* (London, UK: United Bible Societies, 1971) 180.

21 Reid, Thomas. *An Inquiry into the Human Mind on the Principles of Common Sense.* (Edinburgh, UK: Edinburgh University Press, 2010) 6.

22 Lewis, C. S. *God in The Dock.* (Grand Rapids, MI: Eerdmans Press, 2014)

23 Boa, Kenneth, and Robert Bowman, Jr. *Faith Has Its Reasons*. eBook, 2020. https://bible.org/series/faith-has-its-reasons.

24 Craig, William Lane. *Reasonable Faith* (Wheaton, IL: Good News Publishers/Crossway Books, 2009)

25 Doherty, Joe, Elspeth Graham, and Mohammed H Malek. *Postmodernism and the Social Sciences*. (Basingstoke, UK: Palgrave Macmillan, 2001)

26 Hillman, Bruce, "Five Ways Apologetics Can Respond to Postmodernity." https://www.1517.org/articles/five-ways-apologetics-can-respond-to-postmodernity

27 Zacharias, Ravi, *Jesus Among Other Gods* (Nashville, TN: Thomas Nelson Publishers, 2000) 3.

28 Capps, John. "The Pragmatic Theory of Truth". *Plato.Stanford.Edu*. 2020. https://plato.stanford.edu/archives/sum2019/entries/truth-pragmatic/.

29 Roberts, Robert Campbell. *Spiritual Emotions: A Psychology of Christian Virtues*. (Grand Rapids, MI: Eerdmans Press, 2007)

30 Bristow, William. "Enlightenment." *The Stanford Encyclopedia of Philosophy*, 2017.

31 The Khan Academy—The Enlightenment. https://www.khanacademy.org/humanities/us-history/colonial-america/colonial-north-america/a/the-enlightenment

32 Ent, Rolf, Thomas Ullrich, and Raju Venugopalan. "The Glue That Binds Us." *Scientific American* 312 (5): 42-49, 2014. doi:10.1038/scientificamerican0515-42.

33 Edey, Mairland, and Donald Johnson. *Reviewing Blueprints: Solving the Mystery of Evolution* (London, UK: Penguin Books, 1989)

34 Ibid.

35 Chotiner, Isaac. "What if Life Did Not Originate on Earth?" *The New Yorker*, July 8, 2019. https://www.newyorker.com/news/q-and-a/what-if-life-did-not-originate-on-earth.

36 Weaver, Rheyanne. "Ruminations on Other Worlds," *statepress.com*. April 7, 2009. https://web.archive.org/web/20110724233755/http://www.statepress.com/archive/node/5745.

37 Ginsburg, Idan, Manasvi Lingam, Abraham Loeb. "Galactic Panspermia," *The Astrophysical Journal Letters*. Volume 868: L12, October 10, 2018. https://arxiv.org/abs/1810.04307v2

38 Cockell, Charles. "Exposure of Photographs to 548 Days in Low Earth Orbit," *The ISME Journal*, Volume 5 (10): 1671-82. May 19, 2011. https://www.nature.com/articles/is-mej201146.

39 Premise Media. "Expelled: No Intelligence Allowed." IMDb. IMDb.com, April 18, 2008. https://www.imdb.com/title/tt1091617/.

40 Flew, Anthony. *There Is A God: How the World's Most Notorious Atheist Changed His Mind* (San Francisco, CA: HarperOne, 2008)

41 Spear, Gene Wilfred. *What Am I?* (Camarillo, CA: Xulon Press, 2007)

42 Einstein, Albert. "A Talk with Einstein" in *The Listener* 54 (1955) p. 123 and *The Expanded Quotable Einstein* (Princeton, NJ: Princeton University Press) p. 202

43 Einstein, Albert. Third Conversation (1948): William Hermanns, *Einstein and the Poet: In Search of the Cosmic Man* (Brookline, MA: Branden Press, 1983), 94

44 Vallery-Radot, René. *La Vie de Pasteur* (Paris, France: Librairie Hachette et Cie, 1901) 209.

45 Letter (9/10 Apr 1599) to the Bavarian Chancellor Herwart von Hohenburg. Collected in Carola Baumgardt and Jamie Callan, Johannes Kepler Life and Letters (New York, NY: Philosophical Library, 1953), 50.

46 Letter to a Dutch Student (2 April 1873), in Charles Darwin and Sir Francis Darwin (ed.), *The Life and Letters of Charles Darwin* (London, UK: John Murray, 1896), 276.

47 Galileo Galilei, Letter to Grand Duchess Christina of Tuscany, 1615.

48 Ramsay, H. G. H. *In Defense of The Realm* (Morrisville, NC: Lulu Press, 2017)

49 Collins, Francis S. *The Language of God* (London, UK: Simon & Schuster, Ltd, 2008)

50 Oberman, Heiko Augustinus. *The Dawn of The Reformation*. (Grand Rapids, MI.: Eerdmans Press, 1992)

[51] Descartes, René. *Key Philosophical Writings* (Knoxville, TN: Wordsworth Editions Ltd, 1997)

[52] Yeh, Allen, and Chris Chun. *Expect Great Things, Attempt Great Things* (La Vergne, OR: Wipf and Stock Publishers, 2013)

[53] Tiner, John Hudson. *Robert Boyle, Trailblazer of Science* (Milford, MI: Mott Media, 1989)

[54] Pascal, Blaise and W.F. Trotter (trans.), Pensées (1670), Section 10. From "Thoughts," collected in Charles W. Eliot (ed.), The Harvard Classics, Vol. 48 (New York, NY: P.F. Collier & Son, 1910) 85.

[55] Feser, Edward, "Modern Biology and Original Sin," *Edward Feser Blog*, September 23, 2011, http://edward- feser.blogspot.com/2011/09/modern-biology-and-origi- nal-sin-part-ii. html.

[56] Wallace, J. Warner. RightNow Media, "Think Like a Detective" series. https://www.right-nowmedia.org/Content/Series/296435

[57] Thorburn, W. M. *The Myth Of Occam's Razor* (Aberdeen, UK: University Press, 1918)

[58] Sagan, Carl. *Cosmos* (New York, NY: Ballantine Books, 1985)

[59] Gould, Stephen Jay, "Evolution as Fact and Theory," Florida Atlantic University. http://wise.fau.edu/~tunick/courses/knowing/gould_fact-and-theory.html

[60] Hanegraaff, Hank, *The Farce of Evolution* (Nashville, TN: Word Publishing Group, 1998) 85.

[61] Darwin, Charles. *The Origin of Species by Means of Natural Selection, or, The Preservation of Favored Races in the Struggle for Life* (London, UK: John Murray, 1859)

[62] Lewontin, Richard. "Billions and Billions of Demons." *The New York Review of Books*, 1997.

[63] National Academy of Sciences. *Science and Creationism: A View from the National Academy of Sciences.* 2nd ed. (Washington, DC: National Academies Press, 1999)

[64] "America's Changing Religious Landscape." *Pew Research Center's Religion & Public Life Project.* 2015. https://www.pewforum.org/2015/05/12/americas-changing-religious-land-scape/.

[65] Guinness, Os. *Fool's Talk: Recovering the Art Of Christian Persuasion* (Westmont, IL: Intervarsity Press, 2015)

[66] Pascal, Blaise. *Minor Works,* translated by O. W. Wright. Vol. XLVIII, Part 2. The Harvard Classics. (New York, NY: P.F. Collier & Son, 1909–14) Bartleby.com, 2001. https://www.bartleby.com/br/04803.html

[67] Quoted in Os Guinness, *Time for Truth* (Grand Rapids, MI: Baker Books, 2000), 114.

[68] Cantelon, James. *Theology for Non-Theologians.* (Nashville, TN: John Wiley & Sons, 2009)

[69] Singham, Mano. *The Great Paradox Of Science: Why Its Conclusions Can Be Relied Upon Even Though They Cannot Be Proven* (Oxford, UK: Oxford University Press, 2019)

[70] Eves, Howard. *A Survey Of Geometry, Volume One* (Boston, MA: Allyn and Bacon, 1963)

[71] Gossett, Eric. *Discrete Mathematics With Proof* (Hoboken, NJ: John Wiley & Sons, 2009)

[72] Martin Heidegger. *Introduction to Metaphysics* (New Haven, CT: Yale University Press, 1959) pp. 7–8.

[73] Morris, Henry M. *Many Infallible Proofs.* 9th ed. (El Cajon, CA: Creation Life, 1988) 101.

[74] Regopoulos, M. "The Principle Of Causation As A Basis Of Scientific Method." *Management Science* 12 (8), 1966. C-135-C-139. doi:10.1287/mnsc.12.8.c135.

[75] Cameron, Ross. "Infinite Regress Arguments." *The Stanford Encyclopedia Of Philosophy,* 2018. https://plato.stanford.edu/archives/fall2018/entries/infinite-regress.

[76] *Encyclopedia Britannica.* "First Cause | Philosophy." 2020. https://www.britannica.com/topic/first-cause.

[77] *Encyclopædia Britannica.* "Uniformitarianism." 2020. https://www.britannica.com/science/uniformitarianism

[78] Themelios, Vol. 35, Issue 2, "B.B. Warfield on Creation and Evolution," https://www.thegospelcoalition.org/themelios/article/b-b-warfield-on-creation-and-evolution/

[79] Wald, George. "The Origin of Life," *Scientific American*, August 1954. https://www.amazon.sg/Life-Evolution-Readings-Scientific-American/dp/0716710323.

80 Albert Einstein, Letter to Willem de Sitter, 1917.

81 Einstein, Albert. 1997. "Cosmological Considerations In The General Theory Of Relativity". *The Collected Papers Of Albert Einstein*6: 421-432.

82 Ford, Kenneth William. *The Quantum World: Quantum Physics For Everyone.* Cambridge, MA.: Harvard University Press, 2004)

83 O'Raifeartaigh, Cormac, and Simon Mitton."Interrogating The Legend Of Einstein's "Biggest Blunder."" *Physics In Perspective* 20 (4) 2018. 318-341. doi:10.1007/s00016-018-0228-9. 318-341.

84 Hermanns, William, and Albert Einstein. *Einstein And The Poet: In Search Of The Cosmic Man* (Boston, MA: Brandon Press, 1983)

85 Hawking, Stephen W, A Brief History of Time (New York, NY: Bantam Books, 1988), 139.

86 Answers in Genesis, "Six Evidences of a Young Earth." https://answersingenesis.org/evidence-for-creation/six-evidences-of-young-earth/

87 ibid.

88 ibid.

89 Institute in Creation Research, "Many Earth Clocks Indicate Recent Creation." https://www.icr.org/recent-creation/

90 Thomas, Brian, Institute for Creation Science, "Could One Flood Form Many Rock Layers?" September 28, 2018. https://www.icr.org/article/could-one-flood-form-many-rock-layers

91 MacRae, Andrew, The TalkOrigins Archive, "Polystrate Tree Fossils," 1997, http://www.talkorigins.org/faqs/polystrate/trees.html

92 Oard, Michael and Hank Giesecke, Creation Research Society Quarterly Journal, Vol 43, No 3, 232-240, "Polystrate Fossils Require Rapid Deposition," March 2007. https://www.creationresearch.org/polystrate-fossils-require-rapid-deposition/

93 Debenedictis, Albert, *Evolution or Creation? A Comparison of the Arguments,* Third Edition, (Xlibris, USA, 2014), 119.

94 Koch, April, Study.com, "Conditions of Fossil Preservation: Rapid Burial, Hard Parts, and the Elements," Ch 2, Lesson 7, September 2013, https://study.com/academy/lesson/conditions-of-fossil-preservation-rapid-burial-hard-parts-temperature.html

95 Mortenson, Terry, Answers in Genesis, "Young Earth Creationist View Summarized and Defended," February 16, 2011, https://answersingenesis.org/creationism/young-earth/young-earth-creationist-view-summarized-and-defended/

96 Bird, Mark. *Defending Your Faith: A Twelve Lesson Series on Apologetics*, 2nd edition (Hebron, KY: Answers in Genesis, 2011) 59

97 Ibid, 60.

98 Moreland, J.P. *Scaling The Secular City: A Defense Of Christianity* (Grand Rapids, MI: Baker Academic, 1987)

99 Gamow, G. "Jour," Washington Academy of Sciences, Vol. 32, 1942.

100 *Encyclopædia Britannica.* "Big Bang Model." 2020. https://www.britannica.com/science/big-bang-model

101 Schiller, Jon. *21st Century Cosmology* (Charleston, SC: Booksurge, 2009)

102 Nadis, Steve, *Discover Magazine*, "What Came Before the Big Bang?" October 9, 2013, https://www.discovermagazine.com/the-sciences/what-came-before-the-big-bang

103 Colless, Matthew. *The New Cosmology—Proceedings Of The 16th International Physics Summer School, Canberra* (Singapore: World Scientific, 2005)

104 "5.2 Axiomatic Statements Of The Laws Of Thermodynamics." 2020. *Web.Mit.Edu.* http://web.mit.edu/16.unified/www/FALL/thermodynamics/notes/node38.html#SECTION05224000000000000000.

105 Sanford, John C, and John R Baumgardner. 2008. *Genetic Entropy & The Mystery Of The Genome.* Waterloo, NY: FMS Publications.

Endnotes

[106] Wheeler, Tom. *Transformed Thinking: A Defense Of The Christian Worldview* (Greenville, SC: Ambassador Books, 2020)

[107] "Corrigendum: Many Analysts, One Data Set: Making Transparent How Variations In Analytic Choices Affect Results". 2018. *Advances In Methods And Practices In Psychological Science* 1 (4). doi:10.1177/2515245918810511.

[108] Waldie, Lance. *A Christian Apologetic For Christian Apologists* (Self published, 2013)

[109] Paley, William. *Natural Theology* (London, UK: Wilks & Taylor, 1802)

[110] Darwin, Charles. *The Origin Of Species* (London, UK: John Murray, 1906) 144.

[111] Gitt, Werner. "Dazzling Design in Miniature: DNA Information Storage." Creation Ministries International, December 1997. https://creation.com/dazzling-design-in-minia-ture-dna-information-storage-creation-magazine.

[112] Craig, William Lane. "The Teleological Argument And The Anthropic Principle." 2020. https://www.reasonablefaith.org/writings/scholarly-writings/the-existence-of-god/the-teleological-argument-and-the-anthropic-principle/.

[113] Witt, Jonathan. "Does George Smoot, Nobel Laureate, See Evidence of Design in the Cosmos?" Evolution News. February 2, 2007. https://evolutionnews.org/2007/02/does_george_smoot_nobel_laurea

[114] Geisler, Norman and Frank Turek, *I Don't Have Enough Faith to be an Atheist* (Wheaton, IL, CrossWalk Books: 2004) 76.

[115] Jeffrey, Grant R. *The Signature Of God, Revised Edition* (New York, NY: Crown Publishing Group, 2010)

[116] Greg, Allison. *Historical Theology: An Introduction To Christian Doctrine* (Grand Rapids, MI: Zondervan, 2011)

[117] Patterson, Roger. "Were You There? Pointing To God As Creator," *Answers In Genesis.* 2020. https://answersingenesis.org/evidence-against-evolution/were-you-there/.

[118] Collins, Francis S. *The Language Of God* (London, UK: Simon & Schuster, Ltd, 2008)

[119] Schaeffer, Francis. *He is There and He is not Silent* (Carol Stream, IL: Tyndale House, 1980) 7-8

[120] Ham, Ken. Live Lecture at Ark Encounter, Williamstown, KY, August 7, 2020.

[121] ibid.

[122] ibid.

[123] Plass, Ewald M. *What Luther Says: A Practical In-Home Anthology for the Active Christian* (St. Louis, MO: Concordia, 1959), p. 1523

[124] Homer and Alexander Pope. *Iliad Of Homer, Translated By Alexander Pope* (Mineola, NY: Dover Publications, 1999)

[125] McDowell, Josh. *A Ready Defense* (San Bernardino, CA: Here's Life Publishers, 1993) 45

[126] ibid. 46.

[127] Finley, Moses I. *The World of Odysseus (1978)*

[128] ibid.

[129] *Encyclopaedia Britannica.* "Poetry." 1911

[130] Montgomery, John Warwick. *History And Christianity* (Downers Grove, IL: InterVarsity Press, 1971)

[131] Slick, Matt, Christian Apologetics and Research Ministry, "Is the Bible Reliable?" https://carm.org/is-the-bible-reliable

[132] McDowell, Josh. *A Ready Defense* (San Bernardino, CA: Here's Life Publishers, 1993) 43-55

[133] ibid.

<?> ibid.

[134] Kenyon, Frederic. *The Bible And Archeology* (New York, NY: Harper & Row Publishers, 1940)

[135] McDowell, Josh. *A Ready Defense* (San Bernardino, CA: Here's Life Publishers, 1993) 45

[136] North American Review (Oxford, UK: Oxford University Press, 1867) 305

137 Chaffey, Tim. "Unity Of The Bible." Answers In Genesis. 2011 https://answersingenesis.org/the-word-of-god/3-unity-of-the-bible/.

138 Bell, Sheri. "Is The Bible Fact Or Fiction?," 2020. https://www.josh.org/is-the-bible-fact-or-fiction/.

139 Gottschalk, Louis. *Understanding History* (New York, NY: Alfred A. Knopf, 1950)

140 Sanders, E. P. *The Historical Figure Of Jesus* (New York, NY: Penguin Books, 1996)

141 Gudgel, David. *Owner's Guide To Using Your Bible* (Camarillo, CA: Xulon Press, 2009)

142 Williams, Craig. *Is There Evidence For The Christian Faith?* (Camarillo, CA: Xulon Press, 2001)

143 Little, Paul E. *Know Why You Believe* (Westmont, IL: InterVarsity Press, 2009)

144 Glueck, Nelson. *Rivers In The Desert* (New York, NY: Grove Press, 1959)

145 Morris, Henry. *Many Infallible Proofs* (Green Forest, AR: Master Books, 2000)

146 McDowell, Josh and Bill Wilson. *Evidence For The Historical Jesus* (Eugene, OR: Harvest House Publishers, 2011)

147 Heward-Mills, Dag. *Basic Theology* (Camarillo, CA: Xulon Press, 2011)

148 McDowell, Josh and Ed Stewart. *The Disconnected Generation* (Nashville, TN: Thomas Nelson Publishers, 2000)

149 Holden, Joseph and Norman Geisler, *The Popular Handbook of Archeology and the Bible*, (Eugene, OR: Harvest House Publishers, 2013) 89

150 McDowell, Josh. *A Ready Defense* (San Bernardino, CA: Here's Life Publishers, 1993) 176

151 Keaster, Ric. *In Our Own Language: Personality Types And The Gospel Writers* (Tampa, FL: DeWard Publishing, 2013)

152 Morris, Henry. *Many Infallible Proofs* (Green Forest, AR: Master Books, 2000)

153 Rhodes, Ron. *The Big Book Of Bible Answers* (Eugene, OR: Harvest House Publishers, 2013)

154 Harris, R. Laird. *Inspiration And Canonicity Of The Scriptures* (Eugene, OR: Wipf & Stock, 2008)

155 Little, Paul E. *Know Why You Believe* (Westmont, IL: InterVarsity Press. 2009) 65

156 Morris, Henry M. *Many Infallible Proofs*. 9th ed. (El Cajon, CA: Creation Life, 1988) 29-30

157 Ibid. 181

158 https://www.newtestamentchristians.com/bible-study-resources/351-old-testament-prophecies-fulfilled-in-jesus-christ/

159 Smyth, Dolores, Christianity.com, "What are the Prophecies about Jesus?" 2020. https://www.christianity.com/wiki/jesus-christ/what-are-the-prophecies-about-jesus.html

160 Stoner, Peter Winebrenner. *Science Speaks*. (Chicago, IL: Moody Press, 1963)

161 Morris, Henry M. *Many Infallible Proofs*. 9th ed. El Cajon, (CA: Creation Life, 1988) 186-193

162 Little, Paul E. *Know Why You Believe* (Westmont, IL: InterVarsity Press, 2009) 35-37

163 Lewis, C. S. *Mere Christianity* (London, UK: Collins, 1952) 54-56

164 Habermas, Gary R. "Ancient Non-Christian Sources," Faculty Publications and Presentations. Paper 39, 1996. http://digitalcommons.liberty.edu/lts_fac_pubs/39

165 Wilson, Bill. *Evidence for the Historical Jesus* (Eugene, OR: Harvest House Publishers, 1993) 31

166 Little, Paul E. *Know Why You Believe* (Westmont, IL: InterVarsity Press, 2009) 36

167 McDowell, Sean and Josh McDowell. *The Unshakable Truth* (Eugene, OR: Harvest House Publishers, 2010) 161.

168 McDowell, Josh. *A Ready Defense* (San Bernardino, CA: Here's Life Publishers, 1993) 242

169 Schaff, Philip. *The Person Of Christ* (New York, NY: American Tract Society, 1913) 94

170 Ibid, 95

171 McDowell, Josh. *A Ready Defense* (San Bernardino, CA: Here's Life Publishers, 1993) 243

172 Towns, Elmer. *Bible Answers For Almost All Your Questions* (Nashville, TN: Thomas Nelson Publishers, 2003)

Endnotes

Pinnock, Clark H. *Set Forth Your Case* (Nutley, NJ: The Craig Press, 1967) 62

McDowell, Josh. *A Ready Defense* (San Bernardino, CA: Here's Life Publishers, 1993) 243

Ibid. 243-244

Lewis, C. S. *Mere Christianity* (London, UK: Collins, 1952) 54-56

Geisler, Norman L, and Frank Turek. *I Don't Have Enough Faith To Be An Atheist* (Wheaton, IL: Crossway Books, 2007) 348

Stewart, Don. *Blue Letter Bible*, "Why Should Anyone Believe In The Miracles Of Jesus?," 2020. https://www.blueletterbible.org/faq/don_stewart/don_stewart_783.cfm.

Smith, Joseph E. *God In 3D.* (Bloomington, IN: Westbow Press, 2012) 61-62

Persaud, Christopher. *Israel Against All Odds* (Grand Rapids, MI: Christian Publishing House, 2019) 93

Stuart, Douglas. Biblical Training, "Lecture 29: Haggai and Zechariah." https://www.biblicaltraining.org

"The Dead Sea Scrolls—Discovery and Publication." 2020. https://www.deadseascrolls.org.il/learn-about-the-scrolls/discovery-and-publication?locale=en_US.

Strobel, Lee. *The Case For Christ* (Grand Rapids, MI: Zondervan Publishing, 2017)

Morris, Henry M. *Many Infallible Proofs.* 9th ed. (El Cajon, CA: creation Life, 1988) 49

Ibid, 88

Idonije, Henry A. *Is Jesus Christ God?* (Bloomington, IN: Xlibris Corporation, 2013) 119

Schaff, Philip. *The Person Of Christ* (New York, NY: American Tract Society, 1913) 33

Francis, James Allan. *One Solitary Life* (Chicago, IL: Le Petit Oiseau Press, 1963) 1-7

Morris, Henry M. *Many Infallible Proofs.* 9th ed. (El Cajon, CA: Creation Life, 1988) 89

National Basketball Association, "Top Moments: Wilt Chamberlain Scores 100 In 1962 Game Vs. Knicks." 2020. https://www.nba.com/history/top-moments/1962-wilt-chamberlain-100-points.

Bird, Mark. *Defending Your Faith: A Twelve Lesson Series on Apologetics*, 2nd edition (Hebron, KY: Answers in Genesis, 2011) 28

Ibid, 30

Morris, Henry M. *Many Infallible Proofs.* 9th ed. (El Cajon, CA: creation Life, 1988) 96

Maier, Paul L. *In The Fullness Of Time* (Grand Rapids, MI: Kregel Publications, 1997) 203

Hickling, S. Ross. *An Evidentiary Analysis Of Doctor Richard Carrier's Objections To The Resurrection Of Jesus Christ* (Eugene, OR: Wipf and Stock Publishers, 2018)

Chaffey, Tim. Answers In Genesis, "The Resurrection Of Jesus Christ: Faking Death," 2020. https://answersingenesis.org/jesus-christ/resurrection/faking-death/

Johnstone, Patrick; Miller, Duane Alexander. *Interdisciplinary Journal of Research on Religion.* 11: 8. "Believers in Christ from a Muslim Background: A Global Census." 2015. https://www.academia.edu/16338087/Believers_in_Christ_from_a_Muslim_Background_A_Global_Census

Thatamanil, John J. *Circling The Elephant: A Comparative Theology Of Religious Diversity.* (New York, NY: Fordham University Press, 2020)

Yale Center For Faith And Culture. "The Same God?" 2010. https://faith.yale.edu/god-human-flourishing/same-god.

Stanford Encyclopedia Of Philosophy, "The Correspondence Theory Of Truth," 2015. https://plato.stanford.edu/entries/truth-correspondence/#:~:text=The%20metaphysical%20version%20presented%20by,conforms%20to%20the%20external%20reality%E2%80%9D.

The American Heritage Dictionary, "True." 2020. https://ahdictionary.com/word/search.html?q=true.

Stanford Encyclopedia Of Philosophy, "Relativism." 2020. https://plato.stanford.edu/entries/relativism/.

203 Barna Group. "Americans Are Most Likely To Base Truth On Feeling," 2020. https://www.barna.com/research/americans-are-most-likely-to-base-truth-on-feelings/.

204 *Stanford Encyclopedia Of Philosophy,* "Hedonism, " 2020. https://plato.stanford.edu/entries/relativism/

205 *Psychology Today,* "Hedonism Doesn't LEad to Happiness," 2020. https://www.psychologytoday.com/us/blog/out-the-darkness/201708/why-hedonism-doesnt-lead-happiness

206 Bird, Mark. *Defending Your Faith: A Twelve Lesson Series on Apologetics,* 2nd edition (Hebron, KY: Answers in Genesis, 2011) 31

207 Willis, Clyde. *The First Amendment Encyclopedia,* "Atheism." https://www.mtsu.edu/first-amendment/article/1318/atheism

208 Orgel, Leslie E. *Trends In Biochemical Sciences* 23 (12), "The Origin Of Life—A Review of Facts and Speculations, " 1998, 91-495. doi:10.1016/s0968-0004(98)01300-0.

209 Darwin, Charles. *The Origin Of Species By Means Of Natural Selection, Or, The Preservation Of Favored Races In The Struggle For Life* (London, UK: John Murray. 1869) 424

210 Lindsay, Dennis Gordon. *Foundations For Creationism* (Dallas, TX: Christ for the Nations, 1990)

211 Darwin, Charles. *The Origin Of Species By Means Of Natural Selection, Or, The Preservation Of Favored Races In The Struggle For Life.* 6th ed. (New York, NY: D. Appleton and Company, 1882) 98

212 ibid, 98.

213 Wysong, R.L. *The Creation-Evolution Controversy: Toward a Rational Solution* (Midland, MI: Inquiry Press, 2006) 416

214 Ullman, Agnes. *Encyclopædia Britannica,* "Louis Pasteur," 2019 https://www.britannica.com/biography/Louis-Pasteur/Spontaneous-generation.

215 "The Law of Biogenesis." Center for Scientific Creation. February 27, 2020. https://www.creationscience.com/onlinebook/LifeSciences4.html.

216 Geisler, Norman L, and Frank Turek. *I Don't Have Enough Faith To Be An Atheist* (Wheaton, IL: Crossway Books, 2004) 75

217 Darwin, Charles. *The Origin Of Species By Means Of Natural Selection, Or, The Preservation Of Favored Races In The Struggle For Life* (London, UK: John Murray,1869) 424

218 Sober, Elliott. *The Nature Of Selection* (Chicago, IL: University of Chicago Press, 2014) 153

219 Neander, Karen. *The British Journal For The Philosophy Of Science* 46 (1), "Pruning The Tree Of Life," 1995. 59-80. doi:10.1093/bjps/46.1.59.

220 Darwin, Charles. *The Origin Of Species By Means Of Natural Selection, Or, The Preservation Of Favored Races In The Struggle For Life* (London, UK: John Murray,1869) 146

221 Behe, Michael. "Irreducible Complexity, Obstacles to Darwinian Evolution," https://lehigh.edu/~inbios/Faculty/Behe/PDF/Behe_chapter.pdf

222 Colson, Charles W. *How Now Shall We Live?* (Wheaton, IL.: Tyndale House Publishers. 2004) 88

223 Morris, Henry M. *Many Infallible Proofs,* 9th ed. (El Cajon, CA: creation Life, 1988) 263-269

224 Rymer, David. Give Me History, "Animals of Ancient Egypt," March 21, 2019, https://givemehistory.com/animals-of-ancient-egypt

225 Rhodes, Frank H. T. *Journal Of The History Of Biology* 20 (2), 1987, "Darwinian Gradualism And Its Limits: The Development Of Darwin's Views On The Rate And Pattern Of Evolutionary Change," 139-157. doi:10.1007/bf00138435.

226 Morris, Henry M. *Many Infallible Proofs,* 9th ed. (El Cajon, CA: Creation Life, 1988) 252

227 ibid, 251-256.

228 Bird, Mark. *Defending Your Faith: A Twelve Lesson Series on Apologetics,* 2nd edition (Hebron, KY: Answers in Genesis, 2011) 72

229 Public Broadcasting System, "Darwin's Diary, Summer 1842-1844," https://www.pbs.org/wgbh/evolution/darwin/diary/1842.html

Endnotes

230 Answers In Genesis, "Common Ancestor Or Common Designer?" 2020. https://answersin-genesis.org/theory-of-evolution/evidence/common-ancestor-or-common-designer/.

231 Morris, Henry M. *Many Infallible Proofs*, 9th ed. (El Cajon, CA: creation Life, 1988) 240

232 Merriam-Webster Dictionary, "Entropy," https://www.merriam-webster.com/dictionary/entropy

233 Little, Paul E. *Know Why You Believe* (Westmont, IL:InterVarsity Press, 2009) 99

234 Almécija, S. *Neuroscience And Biobehavioral Psychology* 3: 299-315, 2016, "Hands, Brains, And Precision Grips: Origins Of Tool Use Behaviors." doi:https://doi.org/10.1016/B978-0-12-804042-3.00085-3.

235 Ham, Ken, *The New Answers in Genesis, Book 2* (Green Forest, AR: Master Books, 2008) 80

236 Morris, Henry M. *Many Infallible Proofs*, 9th ed. (El Cajon, CA: Creation Life, 1988) 254

237 Darwin, Charles. *The Origin Of Species By Means Of Natural Selection, Or, The Preservation Of Favored Races In The Struggle For Life.* London, UK: John Murray, 1869) 133

238 Darwin, Charles. *The Origin Of Species By Means Of Natural Selection, Or, The Preservation Of Favored Races In The Struggle For Life.* London, UK: John Murray, 1869) 138

239 Stonestreet, John and Roberto Rivera. "Why the Idea of Human Exceptionalism Ruffles Feathers," *Breakpoint*, November 11, 2020. https://www.christianheadlines.com/colum-nists/breakpoint/why-the-idea-of-human-exceptionalism-ruffles-feathers.html?utm_source=News%20&%20Commentary&utm_campaign=News&Commentary_Update%2001/14/05&utm_medium=email&utm_content=3919196&bcid=eed9a93b5cbde76eb3e-922824fb907b5&recip=492008460%20.

240 Smith, Wesley J. "About Human Exceptionalism," The Discovery Institute. https://www.discovery.org/human/about/.

241 Morris, Henry. *Many Infallible Proofs* (Green Forest, AR: Master Books, 1988) 127

242 Strobel, Lee. *The Case For Faith* (Grand Rapids, MI: Zondervan, 2000) 29

243 Sacramone, Anthony. First Things, "God on Trial." November 5, 2008. https://firstthings.com/web-exclusives/2008/11/god-on-trial.

244 Ibid.

245 Giberson, Karl. *Science & Spirit* 17 (5), "Darwin's Annie," 2007. 4-5. doi:10.3200/sspt.17.5.4-5.

246 O'Neill, Ann. *CNN*, "The Reinvention Of Ted Turner." 2013. https://www.cnn.com/2013/11/17/us/ted-turner-profile/index.html.

247 "Steve Jobs biography reveals his struggle with religion, faith in God," *Christianity Today*, November 12, 2020. https://christiantoday.com.au/news/steve-jobs-biographer-reveals-his-struggle-with-religion-faith-in-god.html.

248 Groothuis, Douglas. "Steve Jobs, Jesus, and the Problem of Evil," *Christian Research Journal*, Vol. 36, #1 (2013). https://www.equip.org/article/steve-jobs-jesus-problem-evil/.

249 Weiss, Jeffrey. "Steve Jobs: Prophet of a New Religion," Religion News Service, *The Washington Post*, August 20, 2013. https://www.washingtonpost.com/national/on-faith/steve-jobs-prophet-of-a-new-religion/2013/08/20/0ca29178-09d6-11e3-89fe-abb4a5067014_story.html.

250 "New Bio Quotes Jobs On God, Gates, and Great Design," *National Public Radio* (NPR), October 25, 2011. https://www.npr.org/2011/10/25/141656955/new-bio-quotes-jobs-on-god-gates-and-great-design.

251 Powell, Doug. *Holman QuickSource Guide to Christian Apologetics*. (Nashville, TN: B&H Publishing, 2006) 340

252 Mangaldas, Leeza. *Forbes*, "What You Need To Know About The Country's Controversial 'Beef Ban, '" 2017, https://www.forbes.com/sites/leezamangaldas/2017/06/05/indias-got-beef-with-beef-what-you-need-to-know-about-the-countrys-controversial-beef-ban/#-7f68ae1553c2.

253 Gold, Kenneth A. *United States Foreign Economic Policy-Making* (Abington, UK: Routledge, 2019)

254 Little, Paul E. *Know Why You Believe* (Wheaton, IL: Victor Books, 1987)

255 Zacharias, Ravi. "Why Good Things Happen To Bad People?" Lecture. 2018. https://www.youtube.com/watch?v=aHj9EYQqahA.

256 Anderson, Bryan. *Overwhelmed By Grace* (Camarillo, CA: Xulon Press, 2008)

257 Little, Paul. *Know What You Believe*. (Downers Grove, IL: Intervarsity Press, 2003) 109

258 Strobel, Lee. *The Case For Faith*. Grand Rapids, MI: Zondervan, 2000) 37

259 Lewis, C.S. *Mere Christianity*. (London, UK: Macmillan Publishers, 1952)

260 Wallace, J. Warner. RightNow Media, "Quick Shots: Fast Answers to Hard Questions." https://www.rightnowmedia.org/Content/Series/379632

261 Vitale, Vince. RZIM, "If God, Why Suffering?" https://www.rzim.org/read/just-thinking-magazine/if-god-why-suffering

262 Powell, Doug. *Holman Quicksource Guide To Christian Apologetics* (Nashville, TN: B&H Publishing Group, 2014)

263 Milne, Bruce. *Message Of John* (Westmont, IL: Intervarsity Press, 2014)

264 Bible Hub, "The Redemptive End of Affliction," https://biblehub.com/sermons/auth/barlow/the_redemptive_end_of_affliction.htm

265 Lewis, C.S. *The Problem of Pain* (London, UK: The Centenary Press) 1940

266 Suzuki, Koichi, Takeshi Akama, Akira Kawashima, Aya Yoshihara, Rie R. Yotsu, and Norihisa Ishi. 2011. "Current Status Of Leprosy: Epidemiology, Basic Science And Clinical Perspectives". *The Journal Of Dermatology* 39 (2): 121-129. doi:10.1111/j.1346-8138.2011.01370.x.

267 Anderson, Amy. *Forbes*, "Trials Should Make Us Better, Not Bitter," 2013. https://www.forbes.com/sites/amyanderson/2013/04/10/why-me/#29d03c4e6876.

268 "Family Tragedy—The American Colony in Jerusalem." *Library of Congress*. https://www.loc.gov/exhibits/americancolony/amcolony-family.html.

269 Salama, Toni. Chicago, Tribune, "Jerusalem's American Colony," 2020 https://www.chicagotribune.com/news/ct-xpm-2006-12-10-0612090162-story.html.

270 Denison, Jim, Denison Forum, "Does God Redeem All He Allows?" March 24, 2016. https://www.denisonforum.org/columns/daily-article/does-god-redeem-all-he-allows/

271 Pascal, Blaise, *Pensees* (New York, NY: Penguin Books, 1966), 75.

272 Zacharias, Ravi, RZIM, "Think Again," https://www.rzim.org/read/just-thinking-magazine/think-again-deep-questions

273 Ibid.

274 Ibid.

275 Ibid.

276 Bannister, Andy. RZIM, "Aren't All Religions Equally Valid?" https://www.rzim.org/read/a-slice-of-infinity/arent-all-religions-equally-valid

277 Wallace, J. Warner. RightNow Media, "Quick Shots: Fast Answers to Hard Questions." https://www.rightnowmedia.org/Content/Series/379632

278 Religion Facts, "The Big Religion Chart," http://mhs.magnoliaisd.org/ourpages/auto/2014/8/24/59015366/The%20Big%20Religion%20Comparison%20Chart_%20Compare%20World%20Religions%20-%20ReligionFacts.pdf

279 Dare to Share Ministries, "How to Share The Gospel with a Hindu," https://www.dare2share.org/worldviews/hindus/

280 Religion Facts, "The Big Religion Chart," http://mhs.magnoliaisd.org/ourpages/auto/2014/8/24/59015366/The%20Big%20Religion%20Comparison%20Chart_%20Compare%20World%20Religions%20-%20ReligionFacts.pdf

281 Dare to Share Ministries, "How to Share the Gospel with a Buddhist," https://www.dare2share.org/worldviews/buddhists/

282 Religion Facts, "The Big Religion Chart," http://mhs.magnoliaisd.org/ourpages/auto/2014/8/24/59015366/The%20Big%20Religion%20Comparison%20Chart_%20Compare%20World%20Religions%20-%20ReligionFacts.pdf

283 Dare to Share Ministries, "How to Share the Gospel with a Muslim," https://www.dare-2share.org/article/muslims/

284 ibid.

285 Religion Facts, "The Big Religion Chart," http://mhs.magnoliaisd.org/ourpages/auto/2014/8/24/59015366/The%20Big%20Religion%20Comparison%20Chart_%20Compare%20World%20Religions%20-%20ReligionFacts.pdf

286 Dare to Share Ministries, "How to Share the Gospel with an Atheist," https://www.dare-2share.org/worldviews/share-gospel-atheist/

287 L'Abri, "The L'Abri Statements," https://swisslabri.org/the-labri-statements/

288 Capps, Matt, The Gospel Project, "The Importance of the Christian Worldview," October 13, 2013. https://www.gospelproject.com/the-importance-of-a-christian-worldview/

289 Adamson, Marilyn, EveryStudent.com, "Connecting with the Divine," https://www.every-student.com/features/connecting.html

290 ibid.

291 Wallace, J. Warner. RightNow Media, "Quick Shots: Fast Answers to Hard Questions." https://www.rightnowmedia.org/Content/Series/379632

292 Root, Jerry. *Christianity Today*, "What are Christian Apologetics, and How do they Relate to the Gospel Anyways?" June 14, 2018. https://www.christianitytoday.com/edstetzer/2018/june/what-are-christian-apologetics-and-how-do-they-relate-to-go.html

CPSIA information can be obtained
at www.ICGtesting.com
Printed in the USA
BVHW070744060821
613737BV00004B/530